Published in 2019 by Tasting Arizona LLC

Copyright © 2019 Tasting Arizona LLC

ISBN 978-0-578-56812-6

Written by Luke Irvin and Eric Walters
Photography by Luke Irvin
Book Design by Luke Irvin

Printed in Canada

www.thearizonabeerbook.com

The Arizona Beer Book

This book is dedicated to the hard-working people who put in long hours and sleepless nights to run our favorite Arizona breweries. We appreciate everything you do to keep the beer flowing.

Special thanks, also, to Saywells Design and Adam Green for helping to create this book. Thank you to Goodfellas Merch and AZ Pro Prints for helping us produce some of the industry's very finest merchandise. And most importantly, thank you to the breweries covered in these pages for supporting us and sponsoring The Arizona Beer Book.

Foreword

The Arizona craft beer scene is rapidly becoming recognized throughout the country, and even the world. Many of Arizona's breweries are winning awards at national brewing competitions, showing how great the state's craft beers can be. Thanks to Arizona's beer reputation, local breweries have been getting new chances to share their outstanding creations with people around the country. When an Arizona brewery travels for a collaboration beer or has one of their brews shipped beyond state lines, the liquid carries with it a piece of the great state where it was made. With greater availability, an increasing number of people are beginning to understand how special Arizona is, for beer and for so much more. As the number of local breweries steadily increases, and appreciation for small-batch brews widens throughout the state, craft beer fans have never had so many options for enjoying a cold beer. So we created The Arizona Beer Book to shine a light on our craft scene's special players.

This book isn't a "best of" list or a ranking of our favorite places, but a stepping stone for locals and out-of-towners to begin, or to deepen, their relationship with Arizona's breweries. With a featured lineup of 37 breweries, each based in the 48th state, this book showcases a substantial portion of Arizona's beer producers – all with the goal of highlighting their stellar work and sharing knowledge of local brews with more people. Without the support of the breweries in the book, we wouldn't have been able to make this project happen. The Arizona Beer Book truly is an ode to the Arizona beer family and its community-focused mindset. Volume two of the book will feature more amazing Arizona breweries, possibly including some not yet open. For now, we hope you enjoy our current list of places to visit, and their stories.

Table of Contents

The Brewing Process

Making beer is a relatively simple process that goes back to ancient times. Making consistent beer on a larger scale, however, is a completely different story. Modern brewing requires extensive knowledge of chemistry, microbiology, various ingredients, and so much more. To concoct delicious creations, breweries throughout the state and beyond assemble one-of-a-kind systems and recipes, each brewing setup different from the next. With changes in size, equipment, suppliers, and processes, no two breweries are equal. These variations result in a diverse beer market with a range of novel, exciting creations. For example, larger production breweries may have access to some equipment that a smaller brewery may not have, but smaller places can create more one-offs with quicker, fresher turnaround.

A brewing system can say a lot about a place. Some producers have systems designed to make bigger beers (see Scottsdale Beer Company, page 71). Others may incorporate equipment like horizontal lagering tanks, which help produce specific styles. When craft beer fans learn more about the systems that create beloved brews across Arizona, the nuances of each beer begin to shine. For example, at Helton Brewing Company (page 27), the beer is dispensed directly from serving vessels. These vessels reduce beer's movement and maximize the freshness of every last drop. When visitors feel the chill of the room that houses the serving tanks, it becomes much more apparent why every glass tastes so crisp. Many Arizona breweries have tours available, letting consumers appreciate how various producers navigate the journey from ingredients to exquisite craft creations.

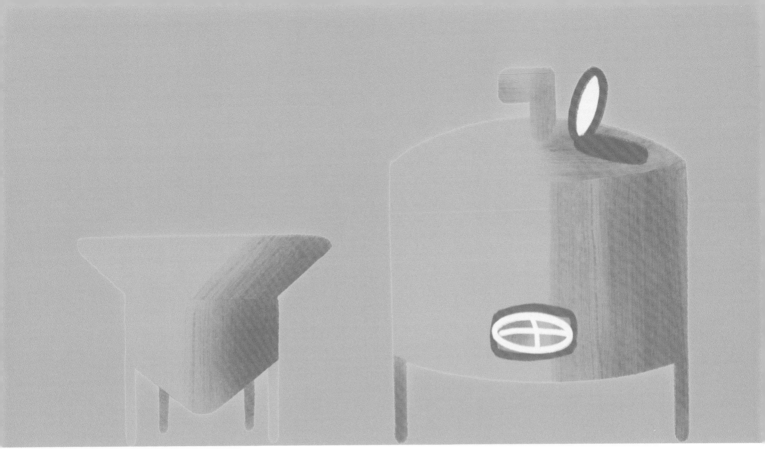

Mill

Putting malted grains through a mill is the first step in the brewing process. By feeding grains through a mill, which cracks open every grain, brewers begin to transform starches into fermentable sugars. Natural enzymes present in the grains make this process possible, but not without a little help from the brewers. Once the grains are cracked, they head over to the mash tun.

Mash

The mashing process affects almost every part of the beer, from color formation, to flavor profile, all the way down to the beer's mouthfeel. While mashing, the grains are soaked in water at a very specific temperature. As the grains are soaked, their sugars dissolve into solution. When brewers mix the grains and water, they create wort, a highly sugary mixture.

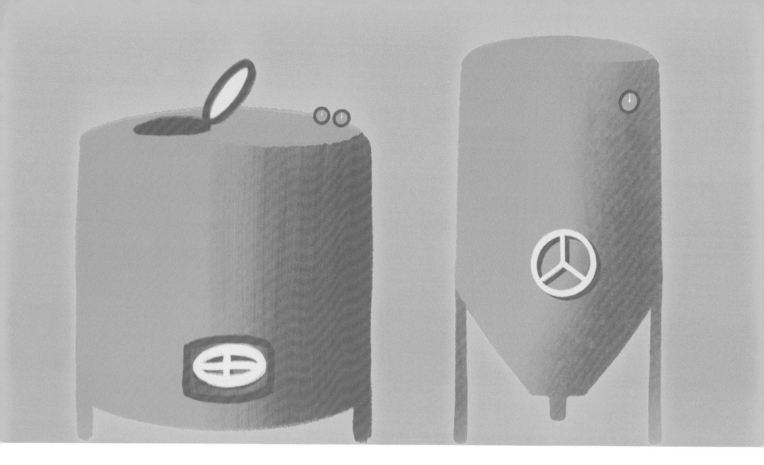

Boil

After brewers transfer wort into the boil kettle, they raise the temperature of the mixture. As this process unfolds, the wort is sterilized, preventing off flavors due to contamination. During the boil hops are added, and the water's heat causes oils in the hops to isomerize. The earlier in the boil that hops are added, the more bitterness they contribute. In contrast, later hop additions will add delicate aromas, like tropical fruit.

Ferment

The real magic of beer happens with yeast. When brewers move wort into fermentation vessels, they pitch yeast, or bacteria, kicking off the fermentation process. During fermentation, the yeast converts sugar into alcohol, as well as a variety of esters that add complexity to beer. The amount of fermentable versus nonfermentable sugars available at this point determines how dry or sweet the final beer will be.

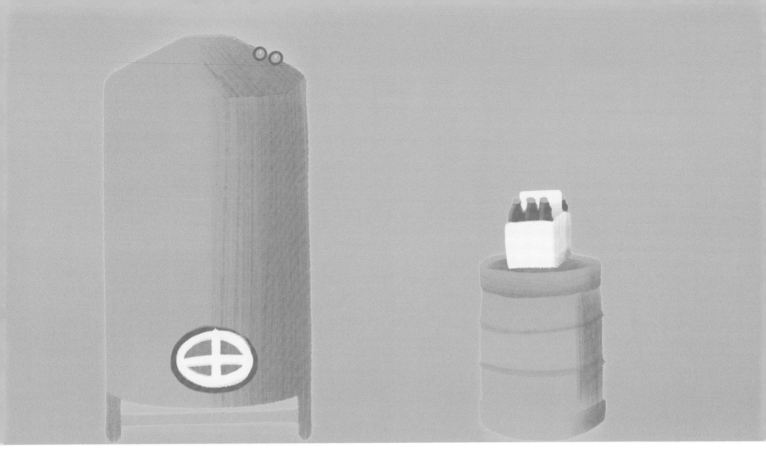

Condition

Conditioning beer is the final stage of preparation before packaging. When beer is conditioned, its temperature is slowly brought down, which causes the yeast to flocculate and fall out of solution. When yeast falls out of solution brewers remove it from the beer, sometimes harvesting the yeast for future batches. Some brewers also carbonate beer at this stage, adding to the mild carbonation from fermentation.

Package

Properly packaging beer is undeniably crucial. Whether in cans, bottles, kegs, or serving vessels, beer is susceptible to a variety of off flavors. Exposure to oxygen and UV light are two of the most common packaging mishaps. To ensure that every drop of beer is fresh, brewers must get their beer packaged and stored with minimal contact to the outside world. Otherwise, the beer's shelf life drastically decreases.

What is Arizona Beer?

Over the past two decades, Arizona craft beer has risen dramatically. In that time, the number of U.S. breweries has nearly quintupled and is on its way to 10,000 nationwide. The growing desire for more intricately crafted food and drinks, along with key legislative changes, has fueled this stunning growth. The craft beer craze first struck areas like Southern California, Denver, and Portland, but the young-and-eager Arizona beer scene has been catching up with a vengeance. In 2011, there were about 35 breweries in Arizona. The state now boasts more than 100 breweries, with new spots

opening all the time. A birds-eye-view of this growth shows enormous benefit to consumers, brewery owners, and their staffs. The beer industry provides tens-of-thousands of jobs across the state and contributes several billion dollars to the economy each year. The Arizona Craft Brewers Guild has played a major role in the success story of Arizona beer, with its crucial support of legislative initiatives such as SB 1030, the Arizona Beer Bill. The Guild also orchestrates popular festivals, conferences, and educational events.

Despite being a young beer scene, Arizona is developing a nuanced craft beer culture of its own. Those involved seem to agree that the goal isn't just to emulate another established beer community, but for Arizona to forge its own path. There is a widely shared mentality that a rising tide raises all ships. In other words, craft beer community members truly support one another, and one party's success lifts everyone else. Some parts of Arizona, such as downtown Tucson and downtown Flagstaff, have groups of breweries clustered in the same vicinity, letting beer fans easily hop from one destination to the next. These walkable districts have become mini beer meccas, benefiting not only all the breweries in the area, but the towns around them.

Instead of businesses forming rivalries, the Arizona beer scene is known for its community. For example, collaboration beers between breweries have become common. These joint beers are brewed all the time, but especially in the run up to festivities like Arizona Beer Week. Events like Real Wild & Woody and Arizona Strong Beer Festival also inspire many breweries to join forces and create brews as a team. Some craft producers even embrace collaborations to get the beer flowing while their brewing systems are still being built. When Old Ellsworth (page 95) opened its doors in 2017, it hadn't actually finished its build-out, so the brewery traveled the state making beer with some of the best breweries in Arizona, including Pedal Haus (page 59) and O.H.S.O. (page 43). Many of the collaborations across the state raise funds for important causes, both inside the industry and out. Cause-supporting creations have been brewed up to benefit everything from medical emergencies to suicide prevention. The Theresa Sorrels Legacy Fund, started by the Arizona Craft Brewers Guild, is one organization that fosters these charitable efforts. The time, money, and care that Arizona breweries give back to their communities is testament to craft beer's positive impact across the state.

Another uplifting attribute of Arizona beer is its strong focus on sustainability and environmentalism. Throughout the state, breweries do tremendous work to help conserve Arizona's natural resources, from sharing spent grains with farmers to reducing water usage. Of course, water is far from abundant in the desert, and beer requires countless gallons every single year. The beer community understands this and does what it can to minimize waste by supporting conservation. Brewery initiatives extend beyond the beer community, often drawing in other organizations to help raise awareness. Nature conservancy groups all over Arizona often team up with breweries like Arizona Wilderness (page 91), Grand Canyon (page 133), and Mother Road (page 105) to further environmental causes that aim to keep the state beautiful.

Where is Arizona Beer?

The best place to experience Arizona craft beer in its purest form is right where it's made – inside a brewery. When the beer isn't transported long distances or held for stretches on shelves or in storage facilities, it's closest to peak freshness. Each step of routing the beer from tanks to a glass increases the possibility of error, which can drastically impact the flavor, potentially diverting beer far from its true character and the brewers' intended experience. Because of this, beer will never taste as good as it does right in its brewery. To keep things fresh, beer producers must take deliberate, precise action, like constantly cleaning draft lines and maintaining exact storage

temperatures. These measures ensure beer won't undergo any unintended changes that could disrupt taste, texture, and appearance. Although trying all of Arizona's best craft beers where they're brewed would be ideal, this isn't always realistic for everyone. Luckily, many other promising options exist for Arizona beer fans to enjoy their favorite beverages, far beyond the brewery walls.

The rise of Arizona craft beer has ignited an explosion of craft beer bars. These gathering places typically feature the same welcoming and laid-back vibe of the breweries that fill their taps, making them a favorite among beer fans. The diversity of brews at craft beer bars can be impressive, spanning all styles, flavors, and parts of Arizona. Teams carefully curate their tap lists, ensuring that customers will be blessed with the best possible options when it comes to sitting down and enjoying a cold pint or two. Craft beer bars often have a to-go retail arm, consisting of fridges filled with all kinds of local cans and bottles. One such place is Tap & Bottle, opened by Rebecca and Scott Safford in 2013. After witnessing and enjoying the growth of Tucson's beer culture, the couple established their first location. Since opening, craft fans in the neighborhood have had prime access to a world of different beers, a selection largely

brewed here in Arizona. Like many craft beer bars, Tap & Bottle collaborates with Arizona breweries, co-creating their own beer for special occasions. Spots like Tap & Bottle also host a steady stream of events, including live music, trivia, and fundraisers, making them a keystone of the Arizona beer community.

A highly practical way to enjoy craft beer is to snag a few bottles and cans from a bottle shop. Destinations like Arcadia Premium in Phoenix don't actually pour beer, but instead specialize in providing cans, bottles, and other to-go craft products. Like beer bars, these retail locations provide an expansive range of options. Customers would be hard-pressed to not find a top-notch brew that matches the style and flavors they crave. "We aim to provide a wide range of products for customers to take home and enjoy," Arcadia Premium co-owner Joel LaTondress says. "Our store offers a comprehensive selection of wine, mead, and even local provisions, alongside our amazing beers." Bottle shops often offer harder-to-find Arizona beers, the rare brews and specialty releases that don't reach the shelves of grocery stores or big-box liquor outlets. Free from the stranglehold of big brands, bottle shops like Arcadia Premium do a standup job of highlighting and supporting local breweries.

For those who enjoy food with their brews, Arizona is a hotbed of restaurants jumping aboard the craft beer bus. Many chefs are now capitalizing on the endless flavors of malt, yeast, and hops, using them to enhance their artful meals, and vice versa. Whether brews are included in the cooking, or as a pairing option with finished plates, beer is becoming more recognized for its beautiful relationship with food. Places up and down Arizona are suggesting food-and-beer pairings on menus. Some even have staff walk customers through the experience. Chefs like Tamara Stanger, who got her start crafting food at a local brewpub, have proven to be creative, new-age culinary talents and the perfect guides for ushering people into today's era of dining with beer. In 2018, she teamed up with Sean Traynor to open Cotton & Copper, a public house focused on Arizona cuisine and cocktails. As a result of her passion for beer, Tamara and the rest of the team, including beer specialist Tiffany Fowler, have built out a local-centric beer menu featuring some of the state's top brewers. Cotton & Copper has even gone so far as collaborating with local breweries like Wren House (page 31) and Arizona Wilderness (page 91), nailing recipes that shine on the restaurant's tap list.

Local Ingredients

One of the most inspiring pieces of Arizona craft beer is the prevalence of projects that promote conservation and sustainability. Breweries use reclaimed water, recycled packaging, and even make direct donations. These efforts have made beer producers local thought leaders, with the impact extending far beyond their brews. While certain projects are more visible than others, much of the preservation efforts begin long before beer is brewed. A handful of local players are making big waves in Arizona (and beyond) by creating sustainable supply chains for breweries and other small businesses. Brewing beer requires a vast amount of natural resources,

including hundreds of gallons of water in every batch. To reduce brewing's impact on the environment, local trailblazers are providing innovative solutions for breweries to harness.

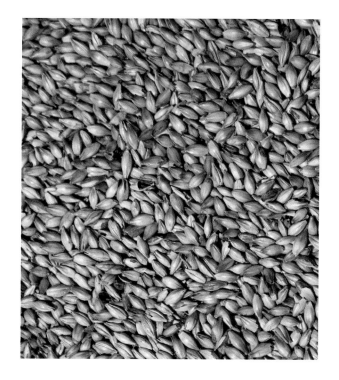

One local champion at the heart of Arizona beer's sustainability efforts is Sinagua Malt. Several years ago, Chip Norton created the company with the goal of channeling craft beer's boom in a way that would benefit Arizona's Verde River. For the past few years, Sinagua Malt has worked directly with farmers to help them grow crops like barley and wheat. Plants like corn and alfalfa are typically grown in the Verde Valley, which are high-water crops that pull more from the Verde River. By helping farmers switch to other crops that use less resources, Sinagua Malt has contributed to the production of tons of sustainable grains here in Arizona. Those grains have since fueled beers from renowned local producers, including Arizona Wilderness (page 91), Wren House (page 31), and other top breweries across the state.

Elsewhere in central Arizona, a prime location for year-round farming, a handful of players are helping conserve the state's natural resources. A great example is Queen Creek's Sossaman Farms, which has been in operation for over 100 years. Over time, this family farm has become synonymous with sustainable practices and innovation. Recently, owner Steve Sossaman helped spearhead the heritage grain movement in the United States. After the movement began to take hold, Sossaman Farms created a new branch of the business called Grain R&D. Since 2012, this seed-to-product organization has focused on cultivating heritage and ancient grains for culinary uses, including bread, spirits, and beer. Heritage grains remain in their most natural forms and have

never been crossbred with other strains. Some local grains fair better in the desert, often using less inputs. Thanks to conscious efforts to restore traditional crops, Grain R&D is adding another level of flavor to Arizona gastronomy, including to fermented products like beer. Brewers love the local aspect of Grain R&D but also appreciate the quality. One of Grain R&D's popular grains, White Sonora Wheat, is a favorite in the brewing community due to the sweetness and soft mouthfeel it lends to beers. Aside from amazing flavor, this grain also makes the brews more environmentally friendly, as White Sonora Wheat requires less water than many modern hybrids.

The diversity of beer styles, flavors, and added ingredients is inspiring brewers to look for more exciting ways to satisfy thirsty, curious drinkers. Now that Arizona brewers are more open-minded than ever, they frequently look to Arizona farmers for novel components they can incorporate. These thrilling ingredients include a wide range of sustainable produce, provided by a network of local growers. Fortunately, farmers across Arizona are cultivating the highest quality produce, only made fresher by their proximity to the breweries. Rhiba Farms, in San Tan Valley, is one of the local producers popular among breweries around the Central Valley. For instance, The Shop Beer Co. (page 53) in Tempe used Rhiba Farm's beets in a special release wit bier, Bohemian Sunshine. Beyond stocking brewers with a range of produce, Rhiba Farms is now experimenting with growing hops, bringing the state's breweries one step closer to the ultimate Arizona beer.

Greg and Kyle Stelzer of 24 Hour Hops are another team of out-of-the-box thinkers spurring the beer revolution. Technology and a growing demand for hops led these two down a path of intense research and discovery. Their experimentation growing greenhouse hops has led to local availability of an ingredient that typically doesn't thrive in the hot Arizona climate. 24 Hour Hops is helping to make locally sourced, wet-hopped beers a year-round possibility. Wet hops are unkilned, so they provide the freshest possible flavors and aromas in beer. In its current phase, 24 Hour Hops mainly provides wet hops to homebrewers. Still, these incredibly small-scale brewers have access to hops previously reserved for larger beer producers. But some Arizona breweries, like SunUp Brewing (page 37), have used 24 Hour Hops in past creations.

Central Arizona Breweries

The most populated hub of Arizona is its capital, Phoenix. Not only does Phoenix have one of the largest metropolitan areas in the United States, it's also home to more than half the state's breweries. With more than 14,000 square miles in the Phoenix metro area, there's a lot of open space for breweries to grow and develop a following. The sheer spread of the beer scene is evident in the 60-plus miles between Saddle Mountain Brewing (page 99) in Goodyear and Old Ellsworth (page 95) in Queen Creek. Though most of the breweries in the Central Valley operate in clusters, not many are within walking distance of one another. To combat this, Arizona Brewery Tours offers guided tours across the Valley, bringing people right to the beer.

Still, areas like Downtown Mesa and Downtown Phoenix are sprouting more and more breweries in walkable areas. Downtown Mesa, for one, is home to Cider Corps (page 79) and Oro Brewing (page 75), with more breweries planning satellite locations in the area. This sets the scene for more cities to evolve into craft beer hotspots in the coming years. Downtown Phoenix has become just that, with Mother Bunch (page 39) making its beers just a short walk from Arizona Wilderness' (page 91) new Roosevelt Row beer garden.

Helton Brewing Company
Phoenix

When entering Helton Brewing Company, a handcrafted barnwood bar presents itself to the sounds of cowpunk playing over the speakers. Fresh beers land across the wooden bar top, beaded with moisture, as bubbles rise up through the liquid gold. Toward the back of the taproom, a large window gives patrons a view of the tall stainless-steel tanks, waiting patiently to create delicious beer whenever asked. Those lucky enough to make a visit to Helton Brewing Company will surely be impressed by the various beers that span the tap list. At any given time, Helton offers four different IPAs and two or three sours, among a handful of other options. Brews at Helton are dispensed directly from serving vessels, as opposed to kegs, which makes for a phenomenally fresh beverage. The founder of the brewery, Brian Helton, comes from a Midwest background, which gives his business a distinct feel.

Special touches, like wood salvaged from a barn back where Brian grew up, adorn the taproom. While living in Ohio, Brian developed his signature take on many beers, including his Valley Venom Pilsner. The flagship Helton brews don't try to be anything special beyond mouthwatering representations of their various styles. Seasonal recipes tend to push the limits a little more. Nevertheless, the Helton methodology is still at every beer's core. Helton often hosts educational events, including brewery tours for those looking to learn more about the craft. Whether patrons are new to Arizona beer or just want to develop a better understanding of the brewing process, Helton's tours are a prime opportunity to dig into the science of beer. Savor pours of Helton brews at their location just up the road from the 51 and Indian School, or on tap and in cans around Arizona.

Valley Venom
Helton Brewing Company

ABV: 4.6%　　　　**IBU: 12**

During his growth as a homebrewer in Cincinnati, Brian Helton found himself surrounded by strong German beer influences. Because of that, the pilsner style was simply a part of his life. So when he first branched out using different yeasts, lagers were a natural fit. Quickly, Brian found himself challenged by the style, as these notoriously hard-to-brew beers don't allow for any flaws. Fundamental components like water chemistry and yeast vitality are even more important for such a delicate beer. If handled improperly, these factors can produce off flavors, which become even more detectable with the mild flavor profile of a pilsner. It has been Brian's mission from the very beginning to create a bright and clean pilsner that stacks up to the centuries-old classics. After nearly two decades of learning and countless modifications, Valley Venom Pilsner has become a centerpiece of Helton Brewing Company. Now, Brian uses this beer as a barometer of his quality. The Pilsner malt, Harrington hop varietal, and lager yeast dictate the taste of this brew. It has a mellow, bread-like flavor with hints of black pepper and floral notes. The refreshing and crisp yet delicate malt character makes Helton's Pilsner the perfect representation of a tasty light beer. The Valley Venom Pilsner is Brian's American adaptation of the classic European style. Therefore, it has a slightly lower alcohol content than a traditional German or Bohemian Pilsner. With its low ABV, Valley Venom is a perfect session beer for all day enjoyment. When pairing it with food, look for more mild flavor combinations like a margherita pizza or grilled chicken. Food paring options at the brewpub include pretzels and beer cheese or a Cuban sandwich, among many other delicious items.

Wren House Brewing Co.
Phoenix

Open since just 2015, Wren House Brewing Company has already become one of Arizona's most renowned beer producers. They have won various local "best of" awards and are starting to turn heads on a national stage. Just as telling is the local fanbase that has come to love Wren House for their well-crafted, sophisticated beers. Wren House always tries to keep a lager on tap, but they also indulge those looking for more specialty brews. Fan favorites frequently include their Triple IPA's and barrel-aged brews. Options like the Wally Series are well balanced and feature flavor profiles that would impress any beer lover. To satisfy their large following, Wren House always pushes the envelope. Some of their exciting projects include legendary collaborations with places like Superstition Meadery. This Phoenix-based brewery has also become a pioneer of can releases in Arizona. Not only are the labels known for being strikingly attractive, people flock from far and wide to swill a taste of the marvelous contents. The beer leads back to head brewer Preston Thoeny, who was brought on when the brewery was first opening. Wren House founders Drew Pool and Bill Hammond convinced Preston to move from his gig in Montana back to his hometown of Phoenix. Now, Preston enjoys pushing his talents to the limit with a relatively large barrel program and a wide range of ambitious recipes. At any given moment, Wren House has around 30 barrels aging and styles ranging from sours to imperial stouts. The taproom on 24th Street is inside of a 1920s bungalow. It was no easy task renovating the old structure into a usable location, yet the results are astounding. The taproom retains many of the building's original features, giving off a clean yet rustic vibe.

Jomax

Wren House Brewing Company

ABV: 6.9%   IBU: 25

Coffee-infused beers often have a strong, unbalanced taste of the bitter breakfast beverage. The Jomax Stout from Wren House Brewing Company breaks this trend in a refreshing way. Roasted whole coffee beans and cold brew layer this stout with a more mellow, reserved coffee essence that gently blends with the beer's sweet malt flavor and velvety mouthfeel. The other ingredients that power this beer include 2-Row Crystal Malt, black malt, and a judicious use of noble hops. Coffee is first added during the boil, when whole roasted beans enter the kettle. After fermenting with American yeast, a second coffee addition is made by way of local cold brew. The result is a deep, rich complexity that makes this beer drinkable year-round, even in a desert summer. From batch to batch, Head Brewer Preston Thoeny can maintain consistency of flavor by modifying the various coffee additions. His use of oatmeal as an adjunct contributes a sweetness that feels natural with the coffee flavor and lets it shine. The protein from the oatmeal helps to build the creamy texture expected in this style of beer. Jomax is one of the oldest brewed beers at Wren House, dating back to before the business opened its doors. In those early days, the crew wanted to create a coffee stout with noticeable oatmeal flavor. Since then, Wren House has completely dialed in this multi-faceted and nuanced brew. It may not be an everyday drinker, but it holds its own beside all the other beers at Wren House. Coming in at nearly seven percent ABV, this beer is sneaky because the alcohol is easily overshadowed by the coffee flavor and oatmeal sweetness. This stout pairs seamlessly with desserts like tiramisu.

SunUp Brewing Co.
Phoenix

Tucked inside a red-brick building on Camelback Road, SunUp Brewing Co. is one of Uptown Phoenix's coziest breweries. Stepping through the front door is a portal to a pristine craft-brew experience: an intimate taproom right next to shiny brewing equipment, separated from drinkers by only a single pane of glass. On the bar top sit classic casks filled with all sorts of intriguing one-off beer combinations. SunUp arose several years back, when John and Sindi Westberg purchased the business. John, a military veteran and architect by trade, designed the brewery as well as the production facility right next door. When SunUp expanded to their new building a few years ago, they boosted their brewing capacity and began to grow their distribution throughout Arizona. Head brewer Uwe Boer stuck around during the transition, enjoying his work making

beer for the quickly growing company. Uwe has been given tremendous freedom to experiment with his brews, which has contributed to SunUp's impressive levels of growth. The cask program at SunUp has been a huge part of Uwe's experimentation, even leading to popular new beers. Casks are traditional serving vessels that can be used to infuse beers with ingredients from coffee beans to fruit, or even just an addition of hops. The beauty of casks is their possible flavors, but they also bring drinkers back to the days before modern brewing techniques like artificial carbonation. SunUp has anywhere between three and eight beers inside the vessels at a time, making for one of Arizona's largest cask programs, if not the largest in the state. Enjoying a glass pulled from the cask is always memorable, as the unfiltered, infused beers take on an entirely new character.

White Russian

SunUp Brewing Co.

ABV: 9.2%   IBU: 65

Nearly thirty years ago, SunUp's head brewer Uwe Boer homebrewed his first Imperial Stout. That same recipe has stuck around to this day and is now the base of White Russian, one of SunUp's most frequent brews. At first glance, White Russian may look like any other dark beer. The color is inky, almost totally black, not allowing any light to shine through its dense body. Coffee and chocolate smells waft from this beer and carry over seamlessly to the flavor. Raisin-like notes of plum are subtle, but entice drinkers until the final sip. Fruity notes are contributed by English Ale yeast, which requires plenty of fermentable sugars to bring this brew to its heady 9.3% ABV. To get the higher alcohol content, Uwe must give the yeast extra time and oxygen, among other inputs. Uwe describes brewing the White Russian Imperial Coffee Stout as "a true labor of love," but the results are absolutely worth the extra work. In fact, the beer has become SunUp's best-selling recipe and is one of the top stouts crafted in Arizona. The cans, which feature an artistic rendering of Uwe, are carried in bottle shops, grocery stores, and convenience stores across the state. Uwe attributes the success of the beer to its complexity and outstanding flavor profile. The integration of coffee, English Yeast, and eight malt varieties creates a unique recipe. Bitterness from whole-bean coffee and sweetness from grains combine to yield flavors reminiscent of dark chocolate. The huge full-body texture adds the final touch that makes this beer so satisfying. Pairing the brew with rich meats like brisket or desserts like chocolate cake highlight the roasted malt flavors, making White Russian even more decadent.

Mother Bunch Brewing
Phoenix

Just past the bustle of Roosevelt Row, stands the magnificent brick building that houses one of Arizona's best brewpubs. Mother Bunch is a restaurant and brewery on 7th Street in Downtown Phoenix, located inside a 100-year-old structure. What was once a popular grocery store, has been painstakingly repurposed as a vessel for downtown's first active brewery. The refurbishing and modernization process made for a tedious reconstruction, but the efforts have paid off in astounding fashion. Mother Bunch has blossomed into a well-rounded producer of both food and beer. This cozy tavern always has a variety of brews, ranging from Pilsners to Double IPA's and Stouts, all crafted right on the urban premises. Mother Bunch beers are often incorporated into the food, providing a spectacular opportunity to pair up a drink with rotating specials or a delectable lunch combo. The business began with the "retirement" of husband-and-wife duo Julie and Jimmie back in 2014. While running a brewery isn't the glamorous task many drinkers dream it to be, the long days can't put a dent in this couple's joy. That delight is evident when the two are posted up at the bar smiling, sharing one of the many beers they've produced. When Julie and Jimmie opened, they wanted to both contribute to the urban culture around them and help make Arizona a national beer destination. Now, the craft beer scene has surged downtown, and Mother Bunch is at the center of its growth. The name Mother Bunch is rooted in history, an homage to the historic alewives who were the original commercial brewers centuries ago. Despite the many changes since the early days of brewing, Mother Bunch has generated a history of its own as a force in Arizona craft beer.

McBride's Irish Red
Mother Bunch Brewing

ABV: 5.4%   IBU: 26

While Mother Bunch has been thrilling downtown drinkers for about 5 years, the recipe for this Irish Red Ale has been making people grin for much longer. Before Julie and Jimmie brewed professionally, they made beer at home for their personal enjoyment. One day, Jimmie decided he wanted a beer with the perfect balance of toasty sweet maltiness and crisp hop character. So after a bit of experimentation and fine tuning, Julie created McBride's Irish Red for her husband. Now, many years later, the brew has become a pillar of the tap list at Mother Bunch. The beer has incredibly clean flavor which greatly contributes to its surprising drinkability. McBride's Irish Red greets drinkers with a mellow yet refreshing bitterness, and is followed by a distinct, roasted flavor reminiscent of high-quality coffee. Even though no coffee is added to this beer, the similar techniques used to roast the malt impart a recognizable flavor on the brew, as well as its darker color. The patent, gorgeous amber hue of McBride's is created entirely by the malts used in the recipe. Due to its lower fermentation temperature, the beer is crisp and clean, without any fruity or ester like flavors. Still, McBride's retains an impressive thirst-quenching capability. Its relative dryness makes it a perfect beer to enjoy with hearty plates of food like fatty meats or the brewpub's cheese board. Mother Bunch even uses McBride's to cook many of their food dishes. It is a great choice for the no frills drinker who prefers a solid beer without any crazy adjuncts or a fancy name. In fact, McBride's has had the honor of being named a finalist at one of the world's most prestigious beer competitions. At just above 5% ABV, it is a perfect choice for those looking for a brew to sip throughout the day.

O.H.S.O.
Phoenix

Whether looking for brunch, an afternoon meal, or a late-night snack, O.H.S.O. is one of the best Arizona breweries to get a bite to eat with family and friends. When founder Jon Lane was concepting the original Arcadia brewpub, he hoped to create a place where the community could congregate – bringing their pets along. Now, his four locations have become hubs for animal lovers looking to hang out with their dogs while they grab a patio beer. Stopping by is always a treat because of the friendly, whimsical atmosphere of the spaces. Several flagship brews will quench craft brew cravings, such as 89 Ale and Lost Viking. They also have several local and regional beers from other skilled breweries. O.H.S.O. always seems to showcase an expansive selection of styles, ranging from lighter beers to porters and stouts. Exciting seasonals, collaboration beers, and even charity brews cycle in on a rotating basis. In fact, about once a month a charitable brew is crafted and put on tap at O.H.S.O. to raise money for donations. Over the years, giving back to the community has become an essential keystone of the business. The good vibes extend to thoughtful programs where organizations like school PTO groups can come in and brew a beer. The benefit – beyond the fun of creating a beer to try later – is that these groups receive all proceeds from tap sales. O.H.S.O. has similar brew-your-own-beer-events for homebrewers and craft beer enthusiasts alike, just another arm of this community-conscious brewery's efforts. This rare experience gives people a special chance to partake in the brewing process, from grain prep to fermentation. All of this is done to bring people together over a pint.

BOOM Dynamite
O.H.S.O.

ABV: 7.0%   IBU: 60

BOOM Dynamite is a perfect patio beer. When considering that O.H.S.O. is well known for outdoor spaces, it's no surprise that this brew is a bestseller. BOOM Dynamite came about as an experimental beer crafted by the brewers, who were looking to develop something they could mostly sip for themselves. But when the first glasses were poured, the brewing team knew they had made something special. Still, they had no idea of the extremely positive response their new creation would get. The brew team was surprised to find out that when the first batch of BOOM Dynamite went on tap, it sold out in a matter of days. This gold rush prompted O.H.S.O. founder Jon Lane to immediately ask the brewers for another batch. The interest from drinkers never died, so the recipe was brought on as a full-time staple. By taking one of O.H.S.O.'s regular IPAs and adding fruit to the recipe, the brewing team accidentally created a brand-new flagship beer. Ever since, this brew has continued to grow its fanbase. The beer itself is made with a pale malt base and a slight addition of wheat. The hop bill includes several varieties used during the boil and after. The real differentiator of this beer, though, is the substantial use of mango and grapefruit, added at the end of fermentation. The bold fruit additions in this recipe create a juicy sweetness and tropical nature unrivaled by most beers. The fruit also lends to the intensely orange, vibrant color of this brew. This highly racchariferous beer is a very easy drinker, even for those who might not typically order an IPA. BOOM Dynamite has caught on in large part because it is so approachable. Such terrific harmony is achieved by building the right amount of bitterness to pair with the fruit-forward flavor.

Walter Station Brewery

Phoenix

Located just north of the Phoenix airport, Walter Station Brewery, opened in February 2019, is one of the state's youngest breweries. Opening was a dream that began to take shape several years ago, when co-founder Kirk Strawn created a community-oriented homebrewing club here in Arizona. At one of the club's meetups, Kirk met his future Walter Station business partner, James Erickson. Naturally, the two homebrewers bonded over several of their own beer creations, then began to entertain the idea of opening a commercial brewhouse. After an extensive planning phase and getting things prepared, the doors of Walter Station Brewery finally opened in a crook of the 202 and 143. Though a newcomer to the maturing Phoenix beer scene, Walter Station has already amassed a sizable local following, with regulars happy to see a new brewery in this part of town. The taproom, housed right between downtown Phoenix and Tempe, fills what was once a fire station. This excellent setting, of course, gives the brewery a ton of character. Walter Station's beers cover a diverse range of styles, offering choices for any palate. Numerous options like the Station Session IPA will satisfy the craft beer enthusiast, but more approachable brews, like the Baja Girl Blonde, are sure to keep any thirsty drinker excited. This blonde ale and Walter Station's other lighter beers have become some of the top sellers since the brewery's recent opening. For those searching to find a rarer brew, Walter Station also pours an ESB and a smoked stout. A food menu is anchored by pizzas, but also includes sandwiches and other small bites. The right combination of hand-crafted food and drinks makes Walter Station a one-stop-shop for serious food and delicious craft beverages.

The Skwincher
Walter Station Brewery

ABV: 4.3%   IBU: 19

As a slightly tart blonde ale, The Skwincher isn't like many other beers. The recipe goes back several years – to a lucky spark of accidental genius by Walter Station's head brewer James Erickson. While toying with his Baja Girl Blonde recipe, James decided to add copious amounts of grapefruit juice and peel. The first batch didn't turn out according to his spur-of-the-moment plan, but it gave James the chance to further experiment with the beer. By adding such a large amount of fruit to a classically light blonde ale, Walter Station formulated a fantastically refreshing recipe, a lush brew kicking with an abundance of tangy flavors and aromas. The Skwincher has quickly risen to the top of Walter Station's young tap list. Its super fresh character and unusual flavor profile even dazzles visitors unaccustomed to drinking craft beer, much to the surprise of the team at Walter Station. This blonde ale has a cloudy opacity which makes it easy to mistake for other, more common styles, like a hazy IPA. But meager use of hops and malt make it as light-bodied and crisp as any other blonde ale. Because of The Skwincher's low alcohol content and fruity freshness, it has an intense summer drinkability surpassing that of most standard, unfruited blonde brews. At about 120 calories per 12-ounce serving, this is a beer that won't make drinkers feel guilty about throwing back a few glasses. As Walter Station evolves, the brewery plans to roll out variants of The Skwincher. One of the alterations in the lineup is a tart cherry version that will offer a slight changeup from the grapefruit option. As with other tangy beers, The Skwincher pairs well with salty dishes or seafood. The sharp flavors in the beer will provide a proper contrast and balance to a delicate fish dish.

The Shop Beer Co.
Tempe

With deep roots in the local community, The Shop is a great place to experience Arizona craft beer. As visitors step into the tasting room, they literally walk into a piece of Arizona history. The building that contains the taproom was constructed in 1952, once housing the mayor of Tempe. More than half a century later, after a thorough renovation, it has become one of the best places in town to grab a fresh beer. To make that transition possible, the founders of The Shop spent several months of blood, sweat, and tears rebuilding the taproom and brewhouse. The hands-on approach was crucial for The Shop, as the custom renovation let the founders create their ideal experience for patrons. When the update unfolded just a few years ago, they set out to create a comfortable environment where people would share beers and spend time. The wooden rafters and exposed ceilings do well to round out the almost living-room-like vibe, tailormade for thoughtful interactions. While drinking beer at this historic location, visitors won't be distracted by a slew of TVs or other forms of entertainment. Instead, there is a natural inclination to engage with other craft beer fans. This sense of fellowship carries over into the brewing. A sizable chunk of The Shop's popular beers are made in collaboration with other breweries. This mentality, common throughout the craft beer scene, is a game changer. When The Shop links up with friends, they tap into each other's skillsets and make brews that never disappoint. The Shop Beer Co. is a must visit simply for its terrific ambiance, and next-level beers like Church Music and F.Y.I.T.M create an experience to remember.

Church Music
The Shop Beer Co.

ABV: 6.7%   IBU: 46

The story of Church Music begins in the early days of The Shop Beer Co., when its founders wanted to create a flagship brew that would be drinkable any day of the year. The Shop also wanted to put their stamp on an IPA market heavily saturated from coast to coast. Many of the IPAs at this time had a potent West Coast style bitterness that turned off drinkers who were just beginning their adventure into craft beer. To appease those new craft drinkers and hardcore IPA fans alike, The Shop created a brew that was balanced and low in IBU, yet still full of flavor. Calling Church Music a juicy IPA is a major understatement. With its bursting, fruit-forward flavor and aroma, this beer is truly an anomaly. The appearance of the brew is so hazy and orange it looks more like a glass of fresh squeezed juice than beer. When closing in for a sip, the overwhelming smell of fresh pineapples and mango jumps right out of the glass. As soon as this beer covers the tongue with its surprisingly full body, a wave of refreshment washes over, bringing excitement and joy to any craft beer lover. Layers of complex tropical flavors evolve throughout each sip, making the brew stand out in the ever-growing list of Arizona IPAs. Now, after a few years of brewing Church Music, this beer has become The Shop's most popular recipe and their fastest growing tap handle across the valley. Aromatic and flavorful hops are the shining star of this recipe, often leaving consumers wide-eyed and smiling. The citrus flavors are not achieved using concentrates or artificial additions, but simply top-notch ingredients, skill, and passion. By adding hops in the late phases of the brew, natural flavors coalesce and showcase their purity, without adding overwhelming bitterness.

Four Peaks Brewing Co.
Tempe

When Four Peaks Brewing Company first began operations in 1996, the craft beer scene was virtually nonexistent; the founders of this Tempe-based brewery had to create a drinking culture in Arizona from the ground up. They chose to do so by focusing on the types of beers they liked to drink: English-style ales. Co-founder Andy Ingram had a strong homebrewing background and spent several years refining his expertise as a commercial brewer at one of Arizona's earliest beer producers, which is where he met the business partners who would eventually help open Four Peaks. When they found their first location on 8th Street in Tempe, Four Peaks' founders immediately knew it was the right place to plant their roots. Built more than a century ago, the former creamery and ice factory required a lot of work to become the brewpub it is today, but its faded brick walls now surround a massive bar at the epicenter of the brewery's empire. As Four Peaks began shipping its beers throughout Arizona and the surrounding states, its reputation and fan base slowly and steadily grew; today, it's one of the most widely known breweries in the Southwest. But reasons for the acclaim go well beyond Four Peaks' position as one of the Grand Canyon State's first craft breweries. Since its inception, Four Peaks has won countless national awards for its fantastic range of beers. Throughout the years, it has also been a key player in the passage of legislative measures that greatly contributed to the growth of the Arizona brewing industry. Alongside brewery mainstays, Four Peaks has an extensive rotating beer list and an impressive food menu – all of which are best enjoyed at the cozy and historic brewpub on 8th Street in Tempe.

Kilt Lifter
Four Peaks Brewing Company

ABV: 6.0%   IBU: 21

Four Peaks' Kilt Lifter has been an iconic Arizona beer for more than two decades. This Scottish-style ale has won a combined seven medals in two of the world's most prestigious brewing competitions and has been a gateway beer for many Arizonans getting into the craft scene. Kilt Lifter's approachable flavor profile, widespread availability, and humorous name have all helped to make the beer the most popular in the state. The recipe was the brainchild of Four Peaks founder Andy Ingram, and was designed to satisfy his itch for a dark, roasty Scottish-style ale. The beer has since become a favorite within the organization and holds a special place in the history of Four Peaks. Decades ago, visitors to the brewery would frequently stop in asking for a beer that tasted like one of the big three domestic lagers. Instead of giving consumers something they expected, Four Peaks' founders made it a point to hand them a Kilt Lifter, which would often be different from any beer they had ever tried. After many years of this kind of introduction to unfamiliar customers, Kilt Lifter has become the cornerstone of Four Peaks' tap list. Indeed, most of the brewery's growth may not have been possible without the success of this Scottish ale. With its signature malt flavor complemented by a proprietary yeast strain, Kilt Lifter has become one of Arizona's most recognizable brews. The resilient English ale yeast provides a very subtle fruity aroma that harmoniously accompanies the roasted malt and hop flavors. Kilt Lifter's caramel-like taste makes it both delicious to drink and versatile to cook with. The chefs at Four Peaks' pubs have incorporated the Scottish ale's smooth, smoky flavor into all manner of dishes. Use the brew at home to make a quick and delicious beer-batter.

Pedal Haus Brewery

Tempe

Pedal Haus Brewery is a gastropub in Downtown Tempe, a stone's throw from Mill Avenue. It sits on a massive lot replete with several bars, a variety of indoor seating, and a giant outdoor patio. The inside is adorned with concrete and steel that fluidly blend into a clean, beautiful industrial design. Outside there is a lush beer garden and lawn games to play, like cornhole and ping pong. When it comes time to order a drink, visitors have multiple world class brews to choose from. Quintessential European recipes are the soul of the Pedal Haus tap list, but seasonal options arise frequently and provide variety. Head brewer Doc Osbourne, who has been crafting beer for decades, has spent his last few years captaining the brew squad at Pedal Haus. When founder Julian Wright first brought Doc into the mix, the mission was clear: Do whatever necessary to make the best beer possible. Pedal Haus has done just that. As a result, the brewery has become a widely respected craft beer destination. Pedal Haus strives to emulate historic brews from all over the world in a way that they consider "true to style." The best example of that mentality might be the Bière Blanche Belgian Witbier, which took home a gold medal in 2018, from one of the world's largest brewing competitions. A good number of Pedal Haus' other beers have won similar accolades at legendary brewing contests, notably the brewery's Valley-renowned American Light Lager. Don't sleep on this brewery's food, either, as the Pedal Haus kitchen utilizes a variety of local ingredients for its refined take on bar food. Dishes range from wood-fired pizza, to fish and chips, and even a Thai Peanut Smoked Salmon salad. Pedal Haus' food, beers, and unreal patio make for the perfect place to throw back a cold one.

Day Drinker
Pedal Haus Brewery

ABV: 3.5%   IBU: 10

Light lagers can be difficult to brew, because they don't contain any in-your-face components that will conceal imperfections. If any one of the ingredients or processes go awry, issues will undoubtedly arise, affecting the taste of the beer. The formation of off flavors like a creamed-corn taste from dimethyl sulfide show up easily in this style. To prevent these problems from happening, head brewer Doc Osbourne must keep an eagle eye on Day Drinker's brewing process. After years of perfecting his recipe, Doc has lifted this beer to new heights. In 2017, Day Drinker Light Lager won silver at the Great American Beer Festival. In the light lager category, Pedal Haus went toe-to-toe with some of the country's biggest breweries, nailing its outstanding showing against some of the most popular beers in the country. When massive macro-breweries produce classic light lagers, they typically add ingredients like corn to increase the alcohol content, without adding any flavor. To put their own fresh craft spin on the light lager, Pedal Haus makes this beer without any adjuncts. By incorporating only 2-row American barley in the recipe, this beer is an outlier in its category. Day Drinker Light Lager from Pedal Haus is the ideal beer to enjoy from afternoon until evening, at long tailgates, or even during a work lunch break. Light lagers typically have a mellow flavor profile and pale-yellow or straw color. According to style guidelines they should have subtle malt and hop flavor. Day Drinker's very low ABV of only 3.5% makes for a thirst quenching, refreshing brew. The neutral taste of this beer balances great with meals like salad or a light sandwich.

Huss Brewing Co.
Tempe

Anyone who knows a thing or two about Arizona craft beer has probably heard of Huss Brewing Co. Huss crafts beers that are both delicious and readily available, making them many peoples first dip into the local beer scene. Huss products are a great embodiment of brewing in the state because they draw so much inspiration from Arizona. Ideas also come from traditional European styles, evident throughout the Huss line of beers. Recipes like Koffee Kolsch show clear German influences. Huss Brewing also ventures into other styles, including a range of IPAs, porters, and wheat ales. One Huss favorite, the widely distributed Scottsdale Blonde, has blown up and become one of the most beloved beers in the state. The company was started in 2013 by the all-star husband-and-wife duo Jeff and Leah Huss. The two had been together for a few years when they decided to start their own family business, using their more than two decades of brewing experience. Building on a true passion for the craft, Jeff and Leah got started in Tempe before more recently expanding to a location in Uptown Phoenix. By now, Huss beers have attained great prevalence and the brewery has a prestigious reputation. The business has become something they would be proud to pass down to their young daughter Lola. Although still too young to imbibe craft beer, Lola has already showcased her entrepreneurial spirit with her own line of Italian sodas, available in both Huss taprooms. Family is the lynchpin of Huss Brewing Co., and it is their goal to share that sentiment with people all around Arizona. One of the brewery's newest beers, Arizona Light Lager, was created so that Arizonans would have a widely available local light lager to enjoy with friends and family.

Scottsdale Blonde

Huss Brewing Co.

ABV: 4.7%	IBU: 16

The Scottsdale Blonde from Huss Brewing Co. is one of the most popular beers in Arizona. It's available in just about any grocery store and can be found on tap in countless restaurants around the state. When Scottsdale Blonde was created back in 2013, it was one of the first beers brewed at Huss. The recipe came about not long after brewery co-founder Leah Huss tried a blonde ale she really enjoyed, but thought could be improved by a slightly sweeter finish. Not long after talking about the beer with her husband, Leah was able to taste the recipe that would become their best-selling beer. Five years after its initial release, Scottsdale Blonde hasn't changed. The beer is modeled after the traditional Kölsch style, brewed across the Atlantic for over a century in Cologne, Germany. By following in the footsteps of the legendary European brewers while adding an American twist, Jeff Huss was able to produce a low-IBU ale with a crisp finish, ideal for the blistering Arizona sun. A light grain bill and sparing use of noble hops make this brew full of flavor while keeping it on the lighter side of the spectrum. The ale yeast used in this recipe is fermented at a slightly cooler temperature, helping to enhance the clean flavor at the brew's heart. The crispness of Scottsdale Blonde is ultimately why people all over Arizona have come to love it so much. Its thirst-quenching goodness and sophisticated, yet approachable flavor profile have been a huge part of its success in the Arizona craft beer scene. One of the special things about Scottsdale Blonde is how great it is for cooking. The Huss family frequently incorporates this brew into recipes for foods like brats or beer can chicken. Scottsdale Blonde's lighter taste will add layers of flavor to meals without adding too much bitterness.

Fate Brewing Company

Scottsdale

For most of his working life, Steve McFate was in the finance business. It was during the tumultuous 2009 financial crisis when he began to think about making a change. The bleak outlook of the financial industry began to spark ideas in Steve's head, including the possibility of opening a brewery. With the help of family and friends, and the fortune of finding an incredible brewer, Fate opened its first location in late 2012. Insert Adam Schmeichel, the head brewer at Fate Brewing Company. Adam has been involved in the Arizona brewing industry since 2012, but he started his career in beer at a brewery in Michigan back in 2007. Before crafting delicious brews, Adam got a formal education graduating from the Culinary Institute of America. He is not only responsible for the amazing beers that Fate quickly became known for, but his culinary background has played a major role in the brewpub's exceptional food menu. Fate features all sorts of delicious food items, including a fan favorite with their wood-fired pizzas. Their wide range of excellent beers supplemented by a quality wine and liquor selection has helped Fate grow into one of Arizona's most renowned food and beer producers. The quality of the brewery's creations is evident in the multiple awards won for various brews over the years. With the success that has taken hold, Fate Brewing Company has expanded to multiple locations, which has become crucial to handling their surging demand. In 2015, Fate added to their original spot with a much larger second location in South Scottsdale. As the company expanded, more people caught wind of their exquisite beers, like the Candy Bar Milk Stout. In 2019, a beautiful third Fate location began operations in Tempe.

Hatch Chile Gatos
Fate Brewing Company

ABV: 4.5%　　　**IBU: 23**

Because of its cream ale base, Hatch Chile Gatos is light in color with a crisp and clean flavor profile. Its gentle malt flavor and mild hop character set the stage for a slightly spicy infusion of Hatch Chiles. The original brew of this recipe took place many years ago in the early days of Fate Brewing Company. During that era of craft beer, there were several popular dark brews enhanced by the infusion of spicy chiles. To create a similar concoction with a refreshing twist, Fate Brewing added hatch chiles to one of their flagship beers. Though it was originally brewed as a one-off, Hatch Chile Gatos occasionally resurfaced with slightly different iterations of the chile pepper component. After repeated success with the beer, Fate decided to keep it on tap as a brewery mainstay. The current recipe is comprised of a simple malt bill, a very slight hop bittering, and a 50/50 blend of mild and hot hatch chiles. The effect of that mixture is a light-bodied, refreshing beer with strong aroma and flavor of green peppers. To ensure the pepper flavor is balanced, Fate Brewing adds roasted chiles to the beer for two whole days at the end of the brewing process. When enjoying this beer at any of the Fate locations, the menu has numerous pairing options. Match this beer with a meal like Fate's Street Tacos to create a regional flavor experience like never before. Fate Brewing even offers patrons the choice to get Hatch Chile Gatos in a michelada style, which takes the beer to a whole new level. For those enjoying Hatch Chile Gatos at home, experiment by using the beer when cooking food. Whether boiling brats or making a beer batter, this brew is versatile in its possibilities, adding sophistication to any dish.

Scottsdale Beer Company
Scottsdale

Who wouldn't enjoy sitting back and watching the big game while drinking a world-class beer? A glass of high-quality suds on a nice afternoon is one of the true joys in life. Add some delicious food to the mix, and that is a blissful combination. Scottsdale Beer Company checks those boxes; a perfect stop for those who want to pair a bite to eat with an award-winning brew. Just off Shea and the 101, this crowd-pleasing brewpub is right in the heart of Central Scottsdale. It is an amazing intersection of food and brews, providing an awesome opportunity for those looking to jump into the Arizona craft beer scene. "People frequently come in for our food and get introduced to our beers" says owner Doug Ledger (pictured on the right). "Our Head Brewer Brad [pictured on the left] is incredibly knowledgeable and does a great job of articulating what he does to create our special beers." The Scottsdale Beer Company brewing system was created specifically for high-gravity recipes. As a result, its brews tend to be big, bold, and full of flavor. Scottsdale Beer Company always has several different styles on tap, covering whatever patrons may be thirsty for. Their signature beers are wildly diverse, ranging from the Big Mouth Blonde Ale to the Dank Triple IPA. Whether searching for lighter beers or hop bombs, this brewery has it covered. The care that Scottsdale Beer Company and its staff have for their food and beer is very apparent. For instance, the various beers always arrive in style-specific glasses to provide the most authentic experience possible. The brewpub is spacious and welcoming, with a superb patio that is perfect for the cooler seasons. When visitors are ready for a change of scenery, they can head to Fate Brewing just a few minutes up the road.

Downshift
Scottsdale Beer Company

ABV: 5.2%   IBU: 55

Session IPAs have been steadily growing in popularity over the past several years. The style has all the hallmarks of other IPAs – mainly a bold hop character and distinct bitterness – but is differentiated by a lower ABV. Back when Scottsdale Beer Company began formulating its recipe for Downshift, they found plenty of session IPAs that were tasty, but most lacked the mouthfeel and rich flavor they craved. So early on in their brewing journey, Scottsdale Beer Company set out to fill a gap in the local market. Downshift has now become one of the defining brews of Scottsdale Beer Company, as well as the fastest-growing IPA they produce. That success has come in large part due to the abundant hop flavor that would satisfy any IPA lover. The Downshift is, of course, lower in ABV than a typical IPA, which makes it a great choice for those looking to enjoy more than a pint or two. To balance the beer's assertive flavor and bitterness, head brewer Brad Williams uses a variety of hops. A clean bittering is achieved using Warrior or Magnum hops, while aromatics are finessed using Centennial and Cascade. Simcoe and Amarillo round things out to create a bright beer with notes of tropical citrus and piney resin. Munich and Caramel malts fine-tune this session IPA with a sweetness that contrasts the hoppy bitterness and helps to create the medium body that Scottsdale Beer Company sought. Since its release early in the brewery's history, Downshift has become one of the producer's staple beers. Scottsdale Beer Company has all sorts of different foods that harmonize with Downshift, including spicy Buffalo wings and fried chicken with Hatch chili sauce. No matter which pairing visitors go with, it will only enhance the already-great ambiance at this brewpub.

Oro Brewing Company
Mesa

In recent years, Downtown Mesa has undergone a major revitalization. All sorts of exciting businesses have opened in the area, from elite sandwich shops to awesome taprooms, galvanizing growth throughout this part of town. The new vitality has arisen in large part thanks to the collaboration between businesses, which have come together to promote the area. One of the organizations at the core of this growth is Oro Brewing Company. With a prime location right on Main Street, this modest spot is perfect for the brewery, as the founders wanted to be in a walkable downtown area since early on. The idea for the brewery germinated when good friends Chuck and Dave realized they wanted to go into business together. Opening a commercial brewery wasn't their first idea, but amidst many long discussions over homebrews, the idea became a reality. It took a handful more years to get the brewery humming, but ever since opening its doors to the traffic and clatter of Downtown Mesa, Oro Brewing Company has had a variety of amazing beers on tap. When these good folks made the transition from home to commercial brewing, they knew they had to bring on some top-notch talent. They found just that in an ambitious young homebrewer by the name of Jesse. Chuck and Dave first ran into Jesse at an Arizona Homebrewing Society event, and they almost immediately decided to bring him on board. Now, even after brewing many thousands of beers at Oro, Jesse truly appreciates his freedom to make delicious brews that appeal to all sorts of different drinkers, both seasoned craft fans and novices. With its relatively small system, Oro Brewing Company can maintain constant freshness across an expansive tap list.

Singularity Series
Oro Brewing Company

ABV: Varies   IBU: Varies

Hops are often the rock stars of a beer recipe. Although malt, yeast, and water play equally vital roles, hops seem to get all the love and glory, and for good reason. Aside from their historically recognized power to extend shelf life, hops provide beautiful aromatics and flavors that other ingredients cannot. The diversity of hops on the market led Jesse Kortepeter, head brewer of Oro, to look for a way he could highlight the unique features of each variety. So when he joined this Mesa brewery in late 2017, Jesse created the Singularity American Pale Ale, a rotating solo-hop series. His hopes were that each time he made a fresh recipe, patrons would be able to experience how a different hop can shape a beer. Oro's single-hop series also allowed the brewery to identify specific flavor profiles present in each of the hops they sourced. The experimental brews now provide valuable intelligence for whenever the brewery crafts a new recipe. The Singularity Series is brewed about once per month using only the freshest hops available. Oro ferments with an American ale yeast to keep the beer crisp and clean while adding a little wheat for lush body. This combination of ingredients leads to an incredibly approachable beer that allows the hops to shine. The different versions of Singularity have covered wide-ranging ground, running the gamut from sweet, citrusy flavors to a resinous, piney character. The drinkability of the pale ale style makes it a favorite among many brewers who want to throw a few back and provides a wrinkle that many IPAs lack. Try Singularity with the breaded chicken sandwich from Worth Takeaway next door, which Oro will let you crush in the taproom.

Cider Corps

Mesa

Brothers Josh and Jason Duren have turned the idea of cider on its head. Over the years that the duo has been serving apple-based beverages in downtown Mesa, they have opened the Valley's eyes to the potential of this beer-like creation. Though cider isn't beer, it is the result of a similar fermentation process. Cider is frequently perceived as a hyper-sweet drink, but this often-underappreciated refreshment has attained a shocking new complexity thanks to the founders of Cider Corps. Several years ago, before the business existed, Josh and Jason found themselves brewing cider to help Jason recover from a traumatic tour in Afghanistan. During the time they spent homebrewing they had a chance to refine their cider making skills on a much smaller scale. Now, their operation has grown into a fixture of downtown Mesa and become a beacon of positivity for veterans of all sorts. Josh and Jason hope that every visit to their location is a chance to Drink Great Cider, Honor Great Sacrifice. As the first full-service taproom of its kind in Arizona, Cider Corps is no stranger to innovation. The crew uses a wide variety of techniques to achieve their delicious flavors. One of the most inventive things that Cider Corps does is incorporate unconventional components into their brews. A quick glance at the constantly rotating draft list will show a culmination of several different ingredients all used in exciting ways. Prickly Pear fruit, pumpkin, tea, and chili peppers are just some of the elements that put the Cider Corps creations in a class of their own. In fact, some of the house favorites feature surprisingly spicy flavor profiles. When visiting the taproom, chances are that patrons will see the Duren brothers sipping something like a honey habanero cider, as they casually mingle with the crowd of visitors.

Purple Heart Cider
Cider Corps

ABV: 6.3%

IBU: N/A

When the original batch of the Purple Heart Cider was brewed the Duren brothers used cascara, the dried skin of a coffee cherry. Cascara is typically thrown away during the coffee harvesting process, though some people use it to make a tea. The story of this unusual ingredient resonated with Jason. When he came home from serving overseas, he was struggling to find a way to share his value. After Jason found cider-making as a hobby it gave him purpose, so the idea of utilizing the cascara in one of his recipes struck him as noble. The cider that emerged was created to honor Jason's Purple Heart from Afghanistan as well as all others who have fought for our country. Jason's injury, passion for cider, and long hours of experimentation have come full circle with this special drink. Unfortunately, cascara can be tricky to acquire, so Cider Corps employs a handful of ingredients that closely mimic the cascara in the original recipe. Morita peppers, which are both smoked and dried, add an interesting sweetness with deep complexity. One of the other ingredients, the Butterfly Pea Flower from southeast Asia, creates the signature color. The vibrant purple hue is the most striking aspect of this cidery's flagship creation, but the flavor profile is just as exciting. The Purple Heart cider has a floral, fruity taste with a slightly dry mouthfeel. The late addition of pears contributes a faint sweetness making for quite a fascinating drink. Luckily, Purple Heart is one of the few ciders that the brothers create all year-round. Cider Corps has also started distributing this recipe to taprooms and restaurants around Arizona. To make this creation even more significant Cider Corps donates a dollar from every glass sold in their taproom to help veterans and their families.

Beer Research Institute
Mesa

This brewpub right off the Superstition Freeway in Mesa is known for beers that are big, bold, and unapologetic. They tend to pack in-your-face flavors and higher ABVs, which separates Beer Research Institute from the average brewery. BRI has always made beers in this heady nature and has no plans to stop anytime soon. These guys have always tried to chart their own path – and are now deservedly recognized for doing so. Whether sipping Morning Sex Milk Stout, 480G IPA, a cream ale, or a fruited sour, visitors are in for a buzzing mouthful of thrills. Buddies Matt Tretheway and Greg Sorrels opened the brewpub back in 2014, with the goal of sharing the types of food and beer they've come to love in more than a decade of brewing together. Ever since their pre-brewpub days of homebrewing, Matt and Greg's go-to style has always been high-gravity beers with generous amounts of flavor and alcohol. From the start, the two found inspiration in music, like 90s hip hop, which gives them a certain swagger and has shaped their anti-establishment vibe. Several years later, they still find themselves creating similar types of beers, just for a bigger audience. Some things have changed since those early days – when BRI was the first brewpub to open in Mesa – like the hiring of a talented head brewer and some expansion of their brewpub. But the objective is still the same: huge beers with style and punch. Beer Research Institute strives to provide a local gathering place where people can sit, chill, and enjoy a delicious beer with scratch-made food. For Matt and Greg, their business isn't about following style guidelines or making trendy recipes. It's just about friends coming together over mouthwatering beer and carefully crafted meals.

480G IPA
Beer Research Institute

ABV: 8.0%

IBU: 71

It's no secret that the founders of Beer Research Institute love their India Pale Ales. From American IPAs to the New England subcategory, Matt and Greg have always been fans of the style. But their favorite IPA is definitely the West Coast version. When brewed with artistry, the West Coast IPA is a loud, assertive beer that smacks the palate with hoppy pungency and bitterness. 480G gains its distinctive hoppy dimensions from dry hopping with two different varieties. An early lush, dank flavor is followed by delicious fruity notes of citrus, mango, and papaya. Careful use of 2-Row and Crystal malt keeps the focus on the hoppy goodness while providing side notes and complexity. The dry finish makes this brew both refreshing and true to style. Its beautiful amber color catches the eye even from across the glossy wooden bar. At 71 IBU, 480G brings potent bitterness, but still maintains an elaborate flavor profile with proper balance. Such a hop forward beer is a perfect choice to pair with a meal. The kitchen at Beer Research Institute makes all sorts of different comfort foods that refuse to be overshadowed by the bitterness in this recipe. Spicy dishes like grilled chicken hot wings or salty bites like pretzel nuggets are a perfect sidekick to a cold pint of 480G. The right food and beer pairing will pleasantly increase the drinkability of this beer and make food much more satisfying. Be careful not to throw back too many 480Gs though. This beer comes in at a strong 8% ABV, which makes it a bigger beer than the average IPA. 480G is available year-round at the Beer Research Institute brewpub (both on tap and in cans) and at several restaurants and bars around the valley.

XWEST BREWING Co.

I 12 Karat	Golden Ale
II 5 Year Plan	Pale Ale
III Peach for the Sky	Hoppy Golden Ale with Agritopia Peaches 5.5%
IV K-Lax	New England IPA 7.2%
V Midnight Run	Oatmeal Coffee Stout 5.3%
VI Idle Essence	Double Dry Hopped Pale Ale 5.8%

VII Frontside	West IPA 7.5%
VIII Ethereal	Hazy Pale Ale 5.8%
IX Zona Pils	Zona Pils 4.3%
X Blap! Blap!	Blood Orange Belgian Wheat 6%
XI Sacrifices	Bourbon Barrel Aged Anisette Imperial Stout 12%
XII Rainbow Dash	Pink Raspberry Lemonade Mixed Culture Sour 3.8%

2019 Beerdevir Calendar $20

Proceeds go to the Theresa Sorrels Legacy Foundation purchase a calendar and get 50% off a pint!

12 West Brewing Co.
Gilbert

12 West Brewing Co. is the product of a shared obsession between co-founders Bryan McCormick and Noel Garcia. Operations started back in 2016, but the journey to get there was many years in the making. The story begins about a decade ago, when Noel was homebrewing beer out of his kitchen. By day he worked as an engineer, and after sunset he got his hands dirty refining his various beer recipes as much as possible. After falling in love with the process of beer production, Noel knew he wanted to open his own brewery. It would take him several years and a few unfruitful projects before he met his current business partner, Bryan. The two quickly bonded while teaming up on some home brewing projects. Not too long after, they decided to go into the brewing business together. That's when things really began picking up. With the help of local legends like Beer Research Institute, Noel and Bryan quickly got their feet under them. Since those early days, 12 West has been pouring brews out of its beautiful taproom at Barnone in Gilbert. Their beers are available elsewhere in cans and on tap throughout Arizona. 12 West is also in the process of expanding to a new location in downtown Mesa right near Oro Brewing Company and Cider Corps. The brewery's flagship fermentations range from the crushable Zona Pilsner to more hop-powered beers, like Frontside West Coast IPA. 12 West also makes more limited brews, including their mixed fermentation line, Cuvée Verdad. Exciting flavor profiles arise when 12 West pushes the limits of beer. They often challenge the conventional by incorporating delicious ingredients like blueberries and other fruits. The Cuvée series has been a large part of their exploration with some releases boasting five different yeast strains.

Zona
12 West Brewing Co.

ABV: 4.3%   IBU: 16

Throughout Arizona and the greater national beer scene, pilsners and other lager-style beers are quickly gaining a devoted fanbase. This might be a response to the super-bitter IPAs of a few years ago, but whatever the cause, the simple, timeless brews of places like Germany and the Czech Republic have burst onto center stage. The drinkability and friendly flavor profiles are magnetic, making brews like these a go-to style for many craft beer lovers. Arizona is particularly ripe for the pilsner style considering the state's incredible heat. So when 12 West created its Zona Pilsner in 2018, it quickly became a fan favorite. The road to this beer's release started long before it was made available to the public. When designing Zona, the 12 West brewing team wanted a great beer to enjoy throughout the day. Still, the brewers wanted to venture beyond the normal pilsner style with a slightly sweeter finish. What 12 West created was a low-ABV beer completed by a full body and round flavors. Being a lager, this recipe must be carefully guided along the way, and the results are worth the extra attention. The Zona Pilsner is perfect as a classic yet new-age sipper, with a ton of flavors and no palate fatigue. The overall taste profile of this brew trends toward the lighter side of the 12 West line up. Expect a beer that is malt-forward with a lasting sweetness and dry finish. Zona's bright, transparent color is a feast for the eyes. Whether soaking up rays on the taproom patio or cooking up barbecue, Zona Pils is the perfect beer to enjoy a great day outside. For those looking to enjoy this beer at home, pair the Zona with delicious meats such as grilled salmon or carne asada. Luckily, the low ABV lets fans enjoy a few beers while keeping on their culinary "A" game.

Arizona Wilderness

Gilbert

Across Arizona stretch deserts, mountains, canyons, and all kinds of natural landscapes that house millions of plants and animals. Pine forests meet towering red rocks and dissolve into the outskirts of a desert laden with coyotes and saguaro cacti. The pristine Arizona outdoors has inspired so many people, including Arizona Wilderness founders Jonathan Buford and Patrick Ware. The bearded business partners are avid outdoorsmen, so from the beginning they wanted to give back to the ecosystems that both support and amaze them. Since 2013, Arizona Wilderness Brewing Co. has been creating internationally recognized beers that help raise funds and awareness for environmentally minded causes. The team at Arizona Wilderness has done all they can to build conservation and sustainability into their brewing business. Much of the malt used at this brewery has been both grown and malted in Arizona. Every single pint purchased from either of the Arizona Wilderness brewpubs contains barley grown within state lines. On top of this, recipes often include next-level components like einkorn, a heritage grain produced locally by Grain R&D. By paying keen attention to their supply chain, Arizona Wilderness Brewing Co. has ensured that everything they do, from their eco-friendly can packs to serving local grass-fed beef, makes the state a better place. Their tap list thrills even the most seasoned craft drinkers, with crazy ingredients like pecan pie, bark, and multiple different wild ales. Arizona Wilderness also frequently works on collaborations with top breweries from around the nation and beyond. The reputation that Jon, Patrick, and the rest of their team has built deservedly precedes them and will no doubt continue to do so.

Refuge

Arizona Wilderness Brewing Company

ABV: 6.8%   **IBU: 65**

Refuge gets its name from a protected strip of wilderness in southern Arizona, just north of Yuma. Much like Refuge's namesake, this brew was created to raise awareness and help preserve the state's natural wonders. By highlighting such a cause while using Arizona grown ingredients, like Sinagua Malt, this beer is a truly excellent local craft. Since it was first brewed nearly a decade ago in founder Jon Buford's garage, this recipe has seen a few changes but remains the same in spirit. These days, Refuge is the brewery's best-selling beer and has become one of the select few non-rotating flagship brews. It is refreshing and crisp with a slight dryness and some sappy notes, reminiscent of the state's great pine forests. A hop-forward character is expected in IPAs, but this beer is way more interesting than a bomb of one-dimensional bitterness. The calculated use of different hop varieties yields a blend of citrus flavors accompanied by a sharp, aromatic evergreen freshness. By focusing on dry hopping, as opposed to additions during the boil, Arizona Wilderness dials back the harshness and draws out the floral flavors of the hop blend. This process makes Refuge more balanced and drinkable. The yeast is the backbone of this IPA, contributing the quiet presence of subtle, ester-like flavors that create complexity. The yeast also adds a slight haziness that permeates throughout this bright orange brew. To put it simply, Refuge is the kind of beer that disappears fast and makes patrons hurry back for another pint. Pair this stellar IPA with one of the grass-fed Arizona Wilderness burgers for maximum deliciousness. Refuge will match perfectly with the salty, fatty burger and won't have a problem standing up to its meaty richness.

Old Ellsworth Brewing Co.

Queen Creek

Starting a new business is never easy. From troubles finding a location to issues obtaining approvals from the city, the brewing industry is filled with stories of hard-won beginnings that can drag on for years. But when an entire community is behind the idea, it can make the whole process a lot easier. In 2016, Queen Creek was looking to add a craft brewery to the area. To fill the void, the city's Economic Development Committee posted an ad in a local magazine. That was when three individuals met the call and opened Old Ellsworth Brewing Company, right on the corner of Ocotillo and Ellsworth Roads. Since operations began, Old Ellsworth proprietors Brian McKean, Christine McKean, and Ryan Bostrom have been sharing their love of craft beer with residents of Queen Creek. The story truly began many years before then, when Brian and Ryan bonded over craft beers. Soon, the two levelled up and started to dabble in homebrewing. Many of those early recipes have now become the base of several Old Ellsworth brews. A strong local focus has led to numerous exciting partnerships with all sorts of Arizona businesses. The brewery sources some ingredients from Grain R&D, just a few minutes up the road, and frequently connects with other breweries throughout Arizona. Collaborations span from Tucson to the northern parts of the state. Old Ellsworth's beers range from saisons to IPAs, with a little something for everyone, even the most hardcore craft beer fans. The food runs from lighter fare like salads to more hearty selections like the Pick-Your-Poutine. With such a comfortable atmosphere to enjoy scratch-made food and drinks, Old Ellsworth has quickly become the much-needed craft brew hotspot that Queen Creek craved.

Winnie's Revenge
Old Ellsworth Brewing Company

ABV: 10%   IBU: 24

The owners of Old Ellsworth Brewing Company have always been fans of an old-school saison. To differentiate this saison from all the other similar beers available around Arizona, they wanted to add a layer of local complexity. Through several experiments, the brewery narrowed in on the perfect combination of ingredients to create Winnie's Revenge, which, yes, nods to the cartoon bear. The recipe begins with White Sonora Wheat, sourced from the local innovator Grain R&D just two miles east of the brewery. To create a beer with a proportionate funkiness, the brewery settled on a Norwegian farmhouse yeast known for its recognizable, but subtle character. The Norwegian flair is not only ideal for the brew, it pays homage to the owners' Viking lineage. To truly set the beer apart, Old Ellsworth adds 150 pounds of local Queen Creek honey to every batch of Winnie's Revenge. This massive amount of honey is all harvested nearby. It's made by bees that migrate between a nearby farm and olive mill every few years. Using ingredients from the area is a major focus of this brew and allows Old Ellsworth to create a special terroir, noticeable in every sip. In the past, the crew has obtained a wine barrel from another Arizona producer in order to create a barrel-aged version of the beer. The slow aging process and barrel itself contribute several flavors, adding dimension to this already superb saison. Due to its uniqueness, the beer has a strong cult following in the taproom. Old Ellsworth's food menu features a few stellar seafood dishes, like glazed salmon, that pair fantastically with this beer. The 10% ABV creates a slightly boozy taste, just barely perceptible on the edge of each frosty sip.

Saddle Mountain Brewing Co.

Goodyear

In 2014, the husband-and-wife duo Laura and Jacob Hansen opened Saddle Mountain Brewing Company. When they started pouring beer at their location right off Route 303 and the I-10, they were the first brewery of their kind to serve Goodyear. Before they got started, this part of greater Phoenix had no brewpubs at all, leaving a gap for the right craft beer producer to step in, bringing fresh beer to town. Laura and Jacob's idea to open the brewery came about after the couple sold a few successful businesses and were contemplating how they should reinvest their money. Laura joked to her husband that they could open a brewery, and from then on Jacob was consumed with the idea. Jacob had spent the previous 15 years learning the process as a homebrewer, so, after some deliberation, they knew it was the right path forward. The duo decided to plant their roots in the West Valley, where they had both grown up. In fact, when Laura was young, she lived just a few miles from Saddle Mountain, the brewery's namesake. Since opening, the two have scored prestigious awards for their beer. Saddle Mountain has a variety of flagship and seasonal brews that will satisfy the newbie or discerning beer lover. Much of Saddle Mountain's inspiration comes from military aviation history – which is why you'll see names like Warhawk (a cream ale) in the brewery's extensive and well-developed Traildragger line of beers. Jacob's love for flying has also led to Saddle Mountain doing a lot of charitable work for the local veteran community. The brewery has a variety of programs that benefit organizations for former service members. Such initiatives are at the core of Saddle Mountain.

Clan Destine

Saddle Mountain Brewing Company

ABV: 6.5% IBU: 21

Scottish style ales are well known for their malt-forward flavor and light hop character. They are typically glassy and transparent, yet marked by a rich, brown hue with a medium body and creamy, off-white head. Saddle Mountain's Taildragger Clan Destine checks all those boxes and measures in at a respectable 6.8% alcohol by volume. What originally began as a seasonal one-off for Saddle Mountain has now become a staple of its tap house. It was just a few years ago, though, that several regulars had to beg for the beer to stay on year-round. Since then, Clan Destine has become one of Saddle Mountain's bestsellers. In addition to the beer's hometown admiration, it has won multiple awards at some of the world's largest brewing competitions. After achieving a gold medal, Clan Destine proved that its reputation is no fluke. The brew is a complex yet drinkable beer that will put a smile on the face of both a longtime craft drinker or someone just getting into the scene. Clan Destine's flavor profile is driven by bready, biscuit-like malty warmth that fades into a subtle, roasted chocolatey finish. Sparing use of hops contributes a very light bittering component that, though faint, drives this beer into perfect balance. In order to best represent the Scottish style, this beer uses ingredients from across the pond. From Simpsons Malt to English yeast, every aspect of this brew is meant to evoke the flavors of historical Scottish ale recipes. The Saddle Mountain brewing philosophy doesn't have room for trendy ingredients or styles. Because of that, they have created a truly refined set of flagship brews. Clan Destine is a superb depiction of what classic beers and excellent ingredients can produce for the sophisticated modern beer drinker.

FLAGSTAFF

ARIZONA US 66

NORTHERN ARIZONA

Northern Arizona Breweries

The pace in northern Arizona is a little bit slower, and those who live and travel there like it that way. Anchored by one of the planet's most breathtaking landscapes, Grand Canyon National Park, northern Arizona is a dream for nature lovers and adventure seekers alike, or simply anyone yearning to experience the state's beauty up close. Places like Flagstaff are major tourist draws, and a perfect stop for the many looking to have a great beer and a bite to eat. Flagstaff is also the main city for a rest before heading into the vast northern Arizona wilderness. This elevated region also serves as a reprieve for Arizonans who need a change in climate, especially during the summer, when Phoenix and Tucson consistently exceed the 100-degree mark.

One of the key factors that makes cities like Flagstaff and Prescott special is bustling downtown areas, friendly urban clusters rich with history, charm, and places to visit. With six local breweries pouring frosty suds in Flag, and a handful more serving thirsty crowds down in Prescott, these towns are truly walkable beer destinations. Cities like Williams and Pine are even mellower than the larger northern Arizona towns, yet each has at least one brewery and plenty of spectacular scenery.

Mother Road Brewing Co.

Flagstaff

Along the edge of the Historic Route 66, where the storied highway cuts through Flagstaff, lies a brew house inspired by Americana and nostalgia. Mother Road, named after John Steinbeck's moniker for Route 66, is a brewery with a classic vibe that nods its head to the golden age of automobiles. References to this era run throughout the business, from the art on the beer cans to the name of the brewery. The tributes to older times stem from a passion within founder Michael Marquess. Back in 2011, when he opened Mother Road, he knew he wanted to pay homage to the amazing history of the brewery's location. Now that Mother Road has expanded to a new taproom and statewide distribution, not much has changed beyond the amount of beer they produce. People have responded not only to the tasty brews, like the famed Tower Station IPA, but also the story that Mother Road tells with each product. Gone are the times when old roadsters would ride the legendary Route 66, yet their memory lives on every time admirers crack open a brew like the Lost Highway Double IPA. Beyond nodding to those who pioneered American automobile culture, Mother Road's purpose is community. Their mission: to brew distinguished beers and build community one pint at a time. This becomes apparent when visiting their tap rooms and experiencing what they call, "Radical Hospitality." It's one of their core values. By that, Mother Road Brewing Co. welcomes all who enjoy craft beer and good conversation to join their growing community. From a bird's eye view, Mother Road's tap rooms are bright and charming, filled with guests of diverse backgrounds. Mother Road hopes that when patrons stop by, they share their unique stories over a nice cold pint.

Tower Station

Mother Road Brewing Company

ABV: 7.3%   IBU: 70

It wasn't until a few years after Mother Road opened that they decided to make an IPA. Back in those early days, the brewery had a somewhat similar seasonal beer, an extra pale ale that the founders one day decided they wanted to evolve into a year-round mainstay. So they created some guidelines for their new beer, including specific grains, hops, and alcohol content. With the help of a new brewer, Campbell, Mother Road began the formulation of its very first IPA. To ensure the team was developing a beer the people would love, the brewery began to recruit the taste buds of everyday customers who stopped in for a pint. After the first few early batches, Mother Road was offering visitors 10-ounce pours of their novel, still-under-construction IPA, asking only for honest tasting notes in return. Each new batch would then implement the feedback, from both customers and the brewers themselves. The collaborative effort that led to the resulting beer, Tower Station, has become a point of pride for the brewery. The name of the beer originates from a trip taken by Mother Road co-founder Michael Marquess, a long ride hauling brewing equipment from Pennsylvania back to Arizona. While driving along Route 66, he passed a popular rest stop known as Tower Station, a place that had lent relief to weary travelers for nearly a century. Michael fell in love with the place and its name, knowing instantly he wanted to use it as the title of a Mother Road beer. Since those fateful days, Tower Station has landed at the top of many "best of" beer lists, not just locally but across the nation. In contrast to resinous or dank IPAs, Tower Station exudes a tropical persona. Pineapple and grapefruit aromas fuse with subtle malt flavor to create an Arizona staple.

Historic Brewing Company
Flagstaff

Back in 2013, John Kennelly, a northern Arizona native, decided he wanted to run his own business. Since John came from a family with multiple successful ventures, including a winery, it seemed like his destiny to follow in the same footsteps. While researching possibilities, John recalled that, many years earlier, his father had flirted with the idea of opening a brewery. After much deliberation, John doubled down on his love of craft beer and bought a commercial brewing system. After an intense update to his new equipment, Historic Brewing Company was born. "The brewery wouldn't have been possible without the success of the restaurants and the support from my parents believing in the dream," John says. In the past six years, Historic has grown to multiple outposts in both Flagstaff and Williams. The brewing operations are still based out of the original facilities in Flag, but these days Historic's reach extends to all corners of the Grand Canyon state. Growth ramped up rapidly when Historic released its locally coveted Piehole Porter. This unconventional brew quickly caught on and became widely available in cans across Arizona. Piehole Porter may be the most well-known Historic beer, but other recipes like Undercover Cucumber are just as pleasing to the palate. A visit to any Historic Brewing Company location will yield a wide variety, as a constantly rotating tap list always keeps visitors intrigued. New pilot beers pop into circulation often, never disappointing. Head brewer Zack Stoll has been with Historic since its earliest days. After spending years rising the ranks, he now stands in the brewhouse's top position. With tens of thousands of cans and kegs distributed monthly, Zack and the Historic team will be busy for the near future.

Piehole Porter
Historic Brewing Company

ABV: 5.5%   IBU: 16

Piehole Porter is one of Arizona's most prominent beers. It's widely available across the state, filling shelves and tap handles from northern Arizona down to Tucson. While this porter is highly regarded, the road to Piehole's success didn't come easy. When the recipe was first created, Piehole Porter was meant to be brewed only once. It was apparent from the outset that the use of cherries and vanilla would greatly complicate the large-scale production of this beer. Compared to all the other beers that Historic brews, Piehole Porter is easily the most tedious to make. Not only is the cherry flavor difficult to extract, but removing the fruit at the end of the process is shockingly time consuming. Despite the difficulty making each batch of this beer, its initial reception was so outstandingly favorable that Historic had to keep making it. After many long brew days and successful releases, Piehole continued to receive ample positive feedback. As the beer grew its fervent fanbase, Historic flourished alongside. At certain points there were occasional hiccups with various aspects, like securing a sustainable vanilla supply. And yet, the brewery persisted in forging its reputation as a delicious beer producer. The unique experience this beer provides is right in line with the thrills that many craft beer lovers constantly seek. Cherry and vanilla additions give the recipe a flavor profile that leans pleasantly into a careful sweetness of rich, dark stone fruit. Still, the beer has a drinkability not often found in this style. Piehole Porter is versatile when it comes to pairing options and can be easily incorporated into food and even other drinks. In fact, Historic uses a reduction of the Piehole Porter to create a special Old Fashioned cocktail at its new bar in downtown Flagstaff.

Dark Sky Brewing Company
Flagstaff

Dark Sky Brewing Company has become known among craft conscious beer drinkers for creating brews that constantly explore new territories and never hold back. Over the years they've been in business, the founders have managed to create beers that perfectly reflect their own eclectic personalities. The crew from Dark Sky truly knows their beer, and often take their knowledge to the next level by doing things like harvesting ingredients themselves. From prickly pear cactus to freshly plucked spruce tips, this Flagstaff brewery is always working to incorporate exciting components. Dark Sky's close relationship with what goes into its beer means that the brews are made using the absolute highest-quality elements and a deep passion for the craft. Dark Sky's taps always flow with new and interesting beers, sporting a selection that is constantly shifting. Since opening in 2015, Dark Sky has brewed hundreds of different recipes, keeping only a few to stand as their tried and true core offerings. On a good week, Dark Sky will release about three new creations, including frequent collaborations with other beer producers like Grand Canyon Brewing Company (page 133) and Beer Research Institute (page 83). For those able to visit Dark Sky, be sure to bring a furry friend along with. The brewery has an animal-friendly patio, ideal for enjoying one of those flawless Flagstaff days. Dark Sky recently partnered up with the skilled local pizza maker Pizzicletta, which now bakes world-class pies right in the taproom. Since the brewery is located in the heart of downtown Flag, there's plenty of fun action within a short walk. After scoring some brews and a bite to eat, why not stroll a few blocks to Mother Road (page 105) or Historic Brewing (page 109)?

Mountains of Mosaic
Dark Sky Brewing Company

ABV: 6.0%

IBU: 93

In recent years, the market for IPAs has drastically shifted. During the early stages of the IPA boom, there wasn't a wealth of options. Lately, IPAs have become quite a diverse style with a slew of sub-categories. Choices range from bone-dry brut IPAs, to more eccentric alternatives, like the creamy milkshake version. However, many beer drinkers prefer to keep things simple with the bitter beauty of a West Coast IPA. Many years ago, Dark Sky's brewers found themselves itching to create a flawless representation of the West Coast style. Around the time they were formulating their recipe, an exciting hop variety called Mosaic was bursting onto the scene. This complex hop provides a range of fruity, floral, and deliciously dank aromas and flavors apt for the clean, West Coast style IPA. Due to its popularity, Mosaic hops were tough to find at the beginning. So

Dark Sky did what any high-flying brewer would do with a limited-supply hop: they threw a "mountain" of it into their recipe. This beer, appropriately named Mountains of Mosaic, pays homage to the soaring Humphries Peak, an iconic highlight of the Flagstaff landscape. The recipe is simple with a subtle malt character that leaves the focus on the beer's star ingredient. A heavy hopping creates a range of flavors that include a pleasant floral component enhanced by citrus and pine aromas. The beer's bitterness is balanced by a dry finish that fades from the palate in a refreshing, lip-smacking manner. As with any other seriously delicious IPA, Mountains of Mosaic pairs great with a rich, cheesy or meaty pizza. Luckily, patrons visiting Dark Sky can snag some Pizzicletta pies that are truly worthy of this uber-refreshing, amazingly aromatic West Coast IPA.

Lumberyard Brewing Co.
Flagstaff

The Lumberyard Brewing Company story began more than 25 years ago, when the Hanseth family came across an article about the up-and-coming brewpub industry. After doing their research, the founders quit their jobs and created Beaver Street Brewery, which is still open today just around the corner from Lumberyard. The couple ran Beaver Street for 16 years before they decided it was time to expand and distribute their award-winning beers. Luckily, they came across a beautiful brick building in the heart of downtown Flagstaff, where the brewpub crafts its delicious beer and food today. The building has quite the past and was a perfect fit for an establishment like Lumberyard Brewing Company. When the original construction was finished in 1890, the structure was used for about 100 years as a lumber storage facility. Once trees were cut down from the surrounding area, they were brought to the building, before being loaded onto trains and shipped off. When Lumberyard Brewing Company moved into the spot, the owners had to invest a substantial amount of time and money to rehabilitate the historical structure. Fortunately, for beer and food lovers alike, the husband and wife duo put in the hard work to make the expansion a reality. The result is a one-of-a-kind brewery sitting beside the train tracks that carve their way through Flagstaff. The brewpub is complete with a patio that views the San Francisco Peaks. When it comes to Lumberyard beers, there are a handful of mainstays and a constant stock of rotating seasonal selections. For those outside of Flagstaff, several of Lumberyard's beers can be found packaged and on tap in towns far from the brewery.

Hazy Angel

Lumberyard Brewing Co.

ABV: 6.7%   IBU: 75

Most of the beers that Lumberyard produces honor styles that have been around for centuries. Several of the Lumberyard recipes have received top regards at major brewing competitions because they follow tradition so well. Options like the Railhead Red, Knotty Pine Pale Ale, and Humphrey's Hefe have been awarded gold medals for deliciously meeting the style guidelines formed over the ages of brewing. While these legendary recipes are successful for Lumberyard, the beer world has brought novel categories, techniques, and flavors. One of the biggest current trends is the relatively new style, the hazy IPA. In a leap away from the beloved classics, Lumberyard recently introduced their take on this novel beer category. Since its release, the new recipe Hazy Angel has won a strong reception and resonated with thousands of Lumberyard fans. The beer has quickly soared to the top of the brewery's tap list and garnered as much success as any of their other options. Hazy Angel was created to answer the call of the masses that love Lumberyard beers, and it has done just that. In the glass, the beer is pale orange and cloudy, releasing a bouquet of tempting sweet, citrusy aromas. Hazy Angel's taste is fruit-forward with the added complexity of a floral hop fragrance and slight bitterness. Lumberyard's taproom has several pairing options that match up fluidly with the Hazy Angel, including a killer Vietnamese burger. This unfiltered IPA isn't challenging to the palate, making it very approachable for newer beer drinkers. Yet at the same time, Hazy Angel delivers enough freshness and nuance to satisfy a true craft beer enthusiast. Lumberyard even donates a portion of the proceeds from this beer to a conservancy organization.

Wanderlust Brewing Co.
Flagstaff

Not shocking given this brewery's name, world travel and the great outdoors are two of Wanderlust's main sparks of inspiration. What's more astounding is the way that founder Nathan Friedman's excursions have influenced his beers. After a trip to Europe, where he experienced the true breadth and culture of beer, Nathan became entranced with the grain-based beverage. Shortly after his interest started to bloom, he was homebrewing all sorts of internationally inspired creations. Now, that passion is the driver of one of Flagstaff's very best breweries. Wanderlust focuses on innovative libations that take Arizona beer down paths less traveled. Many of its beers begin as classic styles but shift toward the southwest through thrilling use of local ingredients, including a wild yeast strain harvested from within the state. Though inspired by travel, Wanderlust beers feature a flavor profile true to their home region. The tap list isn't filled with the typical IPAs, pale ales, or other common beers found at most modern breweries. Wanderlust Brewing Company goes against the grain with recipes that range from eccentric farmhouse ales and saisons to extraordinary gose and other wheat beers. These unconventional brews have set Nathan and his brewery apart while filling in gaps often left open in the market. With beers so far beyond the normal, a visit to Wanderlust Brewing Company takes patrons on a flavor journey much like the trips that galvanized Nathan to open his brewery in the first place. Wanderlust's taproom is located just outside of downtown Flagstaff, right off the historic Route 66 Highway. No more than five minutes away from numerous other Northern Arizona breweries, Wanderlust is a must-stop on the illustrious Flagstaff beer trek.

928 Local

Wanderlust Brewing Company

ABV: 8.0%

IBU: 23

928 Local has one of the most eye-opening backstories of any Arizona craft beer. It all started when founder Nathan Friedman wanted to create a local saison with a flavor profile that not only reflected the rolling hills of the Old World, but the rugged forests and slopes of Flagstaff – the terroir of Arizona. At the time this big idea was simmering, there was only one commercially available strain of yeast used to create this type of beer. Nathan felt he had to secure a local strain of yeast, which would allow for the kind of funky flavors he craved. So Nathan and a few of his engineering friends got together on a project where they would spontaneously ferment cider they pressed themselves. Once the wild yeast was gathered from the spontaneous fermentation, Nathan channeled some brewer's magic and stabilized a single strain, captured directly from the northern Arizona air. This process is rarely carried out by brewers because it requires an impressive understanding of microbiology. With Nathan's newly acquired "wild" yeast strain he began the creation of his Arizona-spirited saison. He devised a recipe with light malt and hops, which would leave room for the flavors from the locally harvested microbes to shine. Nathan then rounded out the recipe by adding honey from a beekeeper in the Flagstaff area, making the beverage even more complex and local. The resulting brew is a slightly funky and earthy beverage completed by a floral sweetness and dry finish. This beer is loaded full of flavors not found in many styles outside of the wild ale category. Of the hundreds of brews created up and down the state, not many Arizona beers boast a local flavor like this one can.

SKOOL HOUSE KOLSCH $6   27 IBU
GROOM CREEK FIRE DEPT COLLAB   5.5%

CORTEZ ST. $5   6%
BLONDE   19 IBU

GREY DUST $5.50
GRISETTE   4.3%
    27 IBU

SAN MARTIN'S 311 AMBER $6
    6.9%
    33 IBU

BUCKEY'S
IRISH RED ALE $5.50   4.1%
    14 IBU

THE YANK $5.50
ENGLISH BROWN   5.5%

PEAVINE PORTER $6   5.4%
    21 IBU

POINT OF ROCKS $6
HAZY PALE ALE   5.2%
    40 IBU

TUMBLEWEED JUICE $6
BRUT IPA   7.1%
    2.8 IBU

MISSING LINK $6
IPA   6.8%
    69 IBU

WEST SIDE STORY $6
WEST COAST IPA   7.1%
    67 IBU

TATANKA $6   8.5%
DOUBLE IPA   8

BLACK COW $6
MILK STOUT

METHOD ESPRESSO ST

Granite Mountain Brewing
Prescott

The diversity of Arizona begins to shine when traveling beyond the big cities. One of the underrated gems is Prescott, rich with history and a vibrant downtown home to Granite Mountain Brewing. As visitors stroll along Cortez Street, a series of antique shops line the road before arriving upon the craft beer destination. Located inside a century-old structure filled with Old West charm, this brewery and taproom has a distinct sense of character. Wooden floors creak as patrons enter the front door and come to an expansive bar. Behind the brewery, a small patio surrounded by lush greenery invites guests to relax. Granite Mountain Brewing, and its cozy taproom, was opened in 2012 by the husband-and-wife-duo Audra Yamamoto and Damon Swafford. The idea for the brewery sparked after the couple put on a series of homebrew tasting sessions. The ensuing wave of encouragement from friends led Audra and Damon to open Prescott's second active brewery. The tap list always includes a little something for everyone, with a stable of favorites like a blonde, brown, and various IPAs. Seasonals fill out the lineup, offering a range of styles that will keep any craft beer drinker thirsty for more. A true connoisseur should look to the barrel-aged specialty brews, which speak to the caliber of beer made at Granite Mountain. Since the taproom is in Prescott's historic downtown, it is frequented by locals and out-of-towners alike. People can't get enough of the thoughtful brews, fantastic weather, and lively community that make the city so special. Granite Mountain has embraced its neighborhood, from collaborations with other businesses to supporting local groups like the homebrewers club – a nod to the brewery's origins.

The Yank

Granite Mountain Brewing

ABV: 7.4%   IBU: 30

Granite Mountain Brewing founder Audra Yamamoto is a big fan of classic English brown ales. Driven by her taste for this malty, slightly sweet style, she wanted to make sure her brewery had one that people could appreciate. When she and her husband Damon introduced their version of a brown ale, called The Yank, they hit the bullseye. With its rich chocolatey color, fluffy head, and multi-dimensional malt character, this recipe is a craft beer lover's dream. The nutty, toasty flavors help to make The Yank a true representation of the brown ale category. The combination of honey, chocolate, and brown malt varieties are key to building this beer's luscious mouthfeel and impressive depth of flavor. Such a complexity and creamy texture make every pint of the Yank a sensuous experience. There's almost no bitterness from the hops, just enough flavor to harmonize with the beer's sweetness. For the craft beer fans who prefer bigger brews with a little more octane, look for Granite Mountain's imperial version of the recipe, aptly titled Big Yank. By turning up the volume of malt, hops, and yeast – but not replacing any components – this Prescott-based brewery gives consumers a recognizable brown ale with more flavor and a significant boost in ABV. Occasionally, The Yank is barrel-aged, creating an extra tasteful blend with even wilder notes. When moved into whiskey barrels, it soaks up all sorts of nuances from the wood, including a noticeable oaky impact. This brown ale's robust roasted malt character makes it a perfect drink for cooler weather, but it still has so much drinkability that it can be enjoyed year-round on the brewery's patio.

Superstition Meadery
Prescott

People have enjoyed mead since before recorded history. While this fermented honey beverage may not be as widely consumed as it once was, it has been finding a renewed appreciation across the planet. It just so happens that one of the world's most highly regarded mead producers is based right here in the 48th state. Since opening in 2012, Superstition Meadery has grown to international distribution while stockpiling various awards. It all began when founders Jeff and Jen Herbert took a stab at homebrewing. Jen purchased a kit for Jeff, and he immediately fell in love with the search for exciting recipes. From the beginning, Jeff focused on creating novel flavors in his beer and mead. One thing led to another, and soon enough the couple was operating out of their historic taproom in Downtown Prescott. What sets Superstition apart is its use of incredible ingredients, beautifully balanced flavors, and uninhibited creativity. Their galaxy of different creations – including meads, ciders, and even hard seltzers – have become widely respected. While mead and beer are two distinct products, they are closely related in many aspects. A few tweaks are made in the process, but just as wort's fermentable sugars lead to beer, honey's sugars lead to mead. The shared science between beer and mead has allowed Superstition to lock down wonderful collaborations with the nation's top breweries, including local gems like Wren House and Arizona Wilderness. Many local breweries also reuse Superstition's barrels to make exquisite aged beers. Because of these efforts and a flawless product, Superstition Meadery has become a key piece of the craft community.

Berry White

Superstition Meadery

ABV: 13.5%   IBU: N/A

According to co-founder Jeff Herbert, his Berry White mead is "the best thing you've never tasted." With a gold medal at the world's largest commercial mead competition to its name, he has a pretty strong argument. Berry White is a barrel-aged mead that uses honey, raspberry, and white chocolate to create an incredible, rich beverage with detailed layers of flavors. As each sip rolls to the back of the tongue, Berry White coats the palate with lush sensations that evolve until the taste has faded. The Berry White recipe was first produced back in 2014 and instantly caught on. After some minor tweaks, this beverage was refined into a picture-perfect craft creation. One of those adjustments included finding the perfect barrel to age the mead. After plenty of experimentation, Superstition Meadery decided on fresh white oak barrels, for their vanilla and coconut nuances. White oak barrels are so crucial that they led in part to this mead's name. "White" in the mead's name also refers to the addition of white chocolate, which greatly shapes the flavor. The mixture of raspberries, white chocolate, and honey creates a level of decadence that is almost unbelievable. Berry White has a handful of spinoffs, including blueberry, strawberry, and blackberry varieties. Thanks to all the different fruits and aging techniques, the Berry White series has become a true exploration into different flavor possibilities. The taste of sweet, tart berries accompanied by the silky-smooth, barrel-aged flavors put this mead in a class of its own. The backbone of the recipe, honey, still shines alongside the other pungent components. As with any world-class craft beverage, Berry White has a deep complexity. Yet still, Superstition Meadery somehow manages to highlight all the ingredients.

Grand Canyon Brewing Co.
Williams

Grand Canyon Brewing Company is one of Northern Arizona's longest-operating breweries, having begun producing their beers way back in mid-2007. Though the local craft beer scene has evolved greatly since those early days, the appreciation for classic styles is still alive and well. Beers such as the Grand Canyon American Pilsner and Sunset Amber may not be as trendy as other options, but these well-executed brews are what the brand has been built on. Even so, Grand Canyon Brewing has branched out and amassed a diverse portfolio, ranging from wild ales to imperial IPAs. This brewery has executed tricky techniques that are often passed over by many others. These include wild-fermented coolship beers and a top-notch barrel aging program. Grand Canyon is also a frequent collaborator with other breweries from Northern Arizona and the central valley alike. Grand Canyon Brewing's mothership is based in Williams, Arizona, a small satellite city just 30 miles from downtown Flagstaff. Williams is flanked by mountains covered in dense forestry, creating a pure natural beauty that has become a central influence for Grand Canyon Brewing Company. Beers like Trail Hike Session IPA pay tribute to the pristine wilderness that surrounds the town. The Williams location is where Grand Canyon crafts all its products, including a line of spirits currently taking Arizona by storm. Recently, Grand Canyon also opened a new location in Flagstaff. After more than a decade of producing beer, this brewery is still crafting many of the same recipes Arizonans have enjoyed for many years. Look for Grand Canyon beers at eateries across the state, or in cans and bottles at a local grocery store.

American Pilsner

Grand Canyon Brewing Company

ABV: 5.0%   **IBU: 25**

Every time a Grand Canyon American Pilsner is poured, a brilliant foam gathers atop the bubbling liquid, bright white and lush. Inviting aromatics of malt and subtle, herbal hops permeate from this European-inspired beer. To give Grand Canyon's American Pilsner a flavor profile aligned with the pilsners of tradition, ingredients are sourced from across the Atlantic. Munich malts are matched up with multiple noble hops, paying homage to the German ancestry of Grand Canyon Brewing Company's founder. Slightly sweet bready notes from the malt blend with a delicate bitterness to make this beer the ultimate refreshment. It was created early on, so that the brewery could always have a crisp, classic lager on tap. To this day, it has been satisfying patrons with its true-to-style flavor. At only 25 IBUs, this beer is perfect for those who tend to enjoy styles that are softer on the palate. The low ABV has made this beer a favorite for Grand Canyon's brewers when they look for a drink after the workday. Over the years, American Pilsner from Grand Canyon has won a handful of awards from various brewing competitions. It has also caught on around Arizona, with cans, bottles, and tap handles appearing throughout the state. For those able to make it into Grand Canyon Brewing Company's restaurant and taproom, American Pilsner makes a great companion to a host of different foods. Subdued flavor combinations, like those of beer-battered cod, make for the perfect pairing. But there's no going wrong matching this brew up with a salad or light sandwich. Fortunately, it's not hard to track down a six pack of Grand Canyon's American Pilsner far from the brewpub, to enjoy after a nice long hike or simply while relaxing on a beautiful sunny day.

Black Bridge Brewery
Kingman

Tim Schritter was born and raised in Kingman, Arizona. For the longest time, he wasn't very interested in craft beer. One day, when drinking a top specialty brew, Tim's views on beer were totally transformed. His newfound energy and appreciation for craft beer eventually led him to home brew in his dad's garage. Soon, Tim's small-batch creations began to make a name for themselves throughout the Kingman community. As his reach grew, Tim began to explore opening a commercial brewery. He quickly put together plans to establish a location in his hometown, where he would sell his highly coveted creations. Before Tim knew it, he was producing beer and distributing to a handful of accounts. Named after a notorious party spot outside of town, Black Bridge Brewery has become a go-to hangout for Kingman locals. Its growth has been completely organic and helped to fuel a craft beer resurgence in the historic town. Black Bridge's reach now extends farther by the day, with tap handles popping up across Arizona. Black Bridge brews its beer right there at the Kingman facility, where patrons can enjoy fresh creations. The tap list is home to about 20 brews at any one time, with a lineup that rotates through almost every style imaginable. Such a variety of recipes virtually guarantees that visitors will find a beer that suits their fancy. Evil Red is a fan favorite, beloved for its 7.7% ABV and distinct hoppiness. For the adventurous soul, there's Wicked Poison, a 14.2% wheat wine on draft year-round. Tim's goal is to have something for everyone, from the craft explorer to those who yearn for the consistency of their favorite style, and even for the non-beer drinker.

BLACK BRIDGE
Brewery
KINGMAN, AZ | EST. 2013

Evil Red
Black Bridge Brewery

ABV: 7.7%   IBU: 57

With its complex malt character and harmonious hop bite, Evil Red from Black Bridge Brewery is a fascinating beer. Numerous malts give this brew a sophisticated flavor profile and beautiful amber red hue. A rich, roasted sweetness makes this recipe any malty beer lover's dream. As Black Bridge founder Tim Schritter says, "craft beer is about experiencing different flavors." This beer delivers just that. To create such a pleasant beer with an appreciable hop character, Tim employs a unique hopping method called hop bursting. When conducting a hop burst, brewers add most or all the hops right at the end of the beer's boiling process. In doing this, Black Bridge can reduce the total IBUs in the beer, allowing more flavors to emerge from hop additions. Due to this method of hopping, Evil Red falls somewhere between the Red IPA and Imperial Red Ale categories, though with such a high ABV, Evil Red is technically an American Strong Ale. No matter how the beer is classified, this brew is a true pleasure to sip. Over the decade-plus that the Evil Red recipe has been brewed and poured, it has seen a handful of special twists. In an audacious attack on drinkers' taste buds, Tim creates a highly spicy version each year, aptly named Scorched Earth. By adding a slew of chiles including jalapeños, habaneros, ghost peppers, and even the legendary Carolina Reaper, Tim takes Evil Red to a merciless place. Scorched Earth stands out even further due to its impressive 11% ABV. If this specialty brew sounds too crazy to drink, try using it to boost flavors when cooking. Several eateries that carry Black Bridge beers have used Scorched Earth in food, including spicy soups.

THAT Brewery

Pine

At the time of the 2008 market crash, Steve and Tamara Morken had spent the past four years running a restaurant in the small town of Pine. Once tough times hit, the couple realized they had to do something else to ensure the survival of their business. Steve, who already had a love of craft beer and homebrewing, noticed breweries were thriving despite the greater economic downturn. So he did more research and found that communities surrounding breweries were also doing well. The couple then took a crucial research trip to Colorado. After confirming that prosperity seemed to follow craft beer, Steve enrolled in a highly respected immersion course designed to help convert restaurants into breweries. In 2012, the husband-and-wife duo transitioned their eatery into THAT Brewery. Their location in Pine soon began selling beers faster than the small brewing system could handle, so more space was needed. In 2014, THAT Brewery opened its Cottonwood location and introduced a new head brewer, John Scarborough. John had previously spent more than a decade producing fine wine, making him a great fit to create THAT's beer. From early on, THAT Brewery has had a strong community focus, using local ingredients like goat's milk and blackberries. The kitchen even has items that utilize grass-fed beef, raised close to the brewery. With its fantastic food selection and pleasingly varied tap list, the original Pine location is the ideal place to enjoy any one of THAT Brewery's creations. The brew pub is tucked into forestry directly off State Route 87, with lush greenery creating the perfect shady getaway to enjoy carefully crafted beer.

Arizona Trail Ale
THAT Brewery

ABV: 6.0%

IBU: 38

The Arizona Trail is a legendary hiking path that winds its way hundreds of miles, from the southern reaches of the state all the way up to Utah. It passes through a rich diversity of Arizona's climates, including Pine, in Tonto National Forrest. One of the trail's entrances can be found near THAT Brewery's first location. Because of the brewpub's proximity to the trail, the founders were inspired to produce a beer that would help protect the area. Owners Steve and Tamara Morken are avid nature enthusiasts, so they created Arizona Trail Ale to raise funds for conservation of the famous path. Now Arizona Trail Ale has become incredibly popular for THAT Brewery and can be found all over the state. In fact, Arizona Trail Ale was the first THAT beer to be packaged and remains a favorite among both regulars and newcomers. Every can sold shows a map of the Arizona Trail, raising awareness for the trail and showing how many parts of the state it unites. Not only are a portion of the beer's proceeds donated directly to the Arizona Trail Association, but one of the beer's main ingredients is Sinagua Malt, produced in the Verde Valley. Use of Sinagua Malt magnifies the impact of Arizona Trail Ale by helping to protect the Verde River. Hops take the spotlight, but with a payload of background malt flavor, the beer is well-balanced. The piney, hop-forward taste of Arizona Trail Ale pairs well with rich fatty meats, especially lamb and beef. On-point pairing options at the tap room include the NY Steak Burger, made fresh at the pub daily. Head brewer John Scarborough often experiments with Arizona Trail Ale, riffing one-off creations. Past iterations have included a green tea version, which John brews occasionally.

SOUTHERN ARIZONA

TUCSON

Southern Arizona Breweries

Southern Arizona's biggest city is Tucson, home to most of the breweries in this part of the state. Tucson is a city rich with culture and a strong commitment to its heritage. Because of this, the beer in Tucson has a flair of its own. Heavily influenced by Sonoran culture and the regional landscape, it's not uncommon to find a sour beer with tamarind or a wheat ale with prickly pear. Exciting creations like these span the area and have led to Tucson becoming the country's first internationally recognized City of Gastronomy. In fact, evidence shows that Tucson has the longest agricultural history in the U.S. With a walkable brewing scene and a bustling downtown, Tucson offers any places to grab a historically influenced drink and bite to eat.

Outside of the Tucson metro area, adventurous drinkers will find scattered outposts of craft beer, flourishing despite the rough desert climate. A 60-minute drive south of Tucson stands America's most Wild-West town: Tombstone, Arizona. After walking down dusty roads and catching a gun show, visitors and locals alike often quench their thirst with some of the state's best cold beers at Tombstone Brewing Company.

Crooked Tooth Brewing Co.

Tucson

Crooked Tooth Brewing Co., just a short walk from Downtown Tucson, produces some of the most eccentric beers on the Arizona craft brewing scene. That's all thanks to husband-and-wife owners Ben and Julie Vernon, who have a deep passion for creating special, out-of-the-box recipes. The story of Crooked Tooth began many years ago, back when Ben was an avid homebrewer. He would often outfit his house with upwards of eight different beers on tap. Over more than a decade, he sharpened his skills, until he and his wife began to entertain the idea of going pro and opening a brewery. The couple decided to pull the trigger and sign a lease for a building that once housed an old car shop. After a thorough update, the location became home for Crooked Tooth. Much of the gritty character has carried over, creating a very distinct aesthetic in the taproom. The Vernons completed the restoration process on their own, allowing them to make necessary updates while keeping the spirit of the building alive. A hands-on approach to running all aspects of the brewery is one of the things that has set Crooked Tooth apart from the craft pack. Ben and Julie love to put their stamp on everything from interior design to next-level brewing touches, all in service of providing a unique beer experience. Events like Full Moon Brews bring a different vibe than the average brewery. The founders' deep-rooted care for beer and whimsical approach culminate most profoundly in the various Crooked Tooth recipes. Refreshing flavor combinations and local ingredients meet in surprising harmony at this Tucson watering hole. Ben and Julie's goal is to have patrons leave Crooked Tooth Brewing Co. asking themselves, "What in the world did I just drink and why was it so good?"

Sonoran Sour Series
Crooked Tooth Brewing Co.

ABV: Varies   IBU: Varies

Sours, one of the oldest beer styles, have seen major growth in today's craft scene. The category encompasses a wide range of flavors, colors, and sub-categories, making it a favorite among many consumers and brewers alike. Some breweries even make sours a major focus of what they do, embracing the diversity of these tart, refreshing beers. Crooked Tooth is one of Arizona's premier sour producers, with many compelling, tangy choices always ready to be poured. With their Sonoran Sour Series, Crooked Tooth has earned esteem and admiration for a lineup of delicious beers that pay tribute to the flavors of the region. Tucson is renowned world-wide for its historic agriculture and food scene, so after growing up in the area, the Crooked Tooth founders had plenty of inspiration to transform into beverages. Their ideas have now manifested into some of Arizona beer's most imaginative creations. The team at Crooked Tooth has been strongly influenced by the Sonoran culture that surrounds them, which has become a vital component to this locally-driven line of beers. From fruit-powered agua frescas to Mexican snow cones called raspados, all sorts of flavors galvanize the sour brews that appear in this standout series. The Sonoran Sours are truly an exploration in flavor, one that requires Crooked Tooth to keep a close eye on each brew, often making tiny adjustments throughout the fermentation process. Although the entire series is a big hit with fans of the brewery, Cloud People may be the most sought-after of them all. This award-winning sour brown ale is fermented with tamarindo and poured into a chili-lime coated glass, giving it a true essence of the Sonoran Desert. Past brews have also incorporated sensational ingredients, like horchata and jamaica.

Barrio Brewing Co.
Tucson

Nearly three decades ago, Arizona natives Dennis Arnold and his wife, Tauna, opened their first brewery in Tucson. Neither of them had come from a beer background, so the business came with a learning curve. Back in 1991, craft beer was nothing like it is now, so the duo had to carve their own path. To make things work, they had to be resourceful. Much of their business, including their original brewing system, was built totally by hand. From the beginning, the goal was to make drinkable, practical beers that Tucsonans would want to drink year-round. They grew their company for 15 years under the name Gentle Ben's, until space had grown short and it was time to expand. The husband-and-wife team began operating out of a second location called Barrio Brewing Co. in 2006. Post-expansion, not much changed for Dennis and Tauna. Recipes stayed the same, and with improved facilities, the quality only got better. Now, about a decade and a half after they expanded their base, the Arnolds have grown their business on a massive scale. Their flourishing brewery has become the third biggest independent beer producer in Arizona. Despite its enormous size, Barrio Brewing Co. remains a true family business. Dennis and Tauna have been running the operations since the beginning, with many of their employees along for the ride. A fair amount of their staff has been around for a decade or more, which is a testament to what type of business the Arnolds run. The track record for Barrio Brewing Co. speaks for itself. Barrio's beers are known for being classic and satisfying, which is why their popular flagships are available across the entire state of Arizona. As they continue growing, Barrio strives to share their beers with more great Arizonans.

Barrio Blonde
Barrio Brewing Co.

ABV: 4.5%   ### IBU: 14

Barrio Blonde is the oldest Arizona beer recipe to be consistently brewed on a commercial scale. The very first batch was made all the way back on May 1, 1991. Originally dubbed the Tucson Blonde, this brew is a true ode to the Arizona craft beer drinker. When the brewery's co-founder Dennis Arnold was first brainstorming the recipe, his goal was to make something people couldn't resist drinking. So he closely observed his customers. What he noticed was that they tended to opt for a beer that was light, crisp, and refreshing. To satisfy the early wave of craft beer fans in Tucson, Dennis perfected a beer that had all these attributes in spades. Three decades after its creation, Barrio Blonde is one of the smoothest brews in all of Arizona. The beer's unbelievable drinkability has won it a sizeable, loyal fanbase. It has such a following that Dennis has a saying: "Once the blonde goes on tap somewhere, it doesn't come off." People who try Barrio Blonde at restaurants or in cans often find a prime place for it in their regular rotation. To create such a widely enjoyed lighter beer, Barrio Brewing must keep a close eye on the entire production process. A beer as delicate as this one can easily show imperfections that bolder beers might be able to cover up. Even a slight change from one hop harvest to the next can totally transform the flavor profile of this brew. Barrio Blonde's recipe is simple and true, with just one hop variety: the legendary Czech Saaz. Still, this beer is full of enticing flavors and aromas that would excite any craft drinker. Its creamy, bright-white head draws in the eyes, and the beer's thirst-quenching capability keeps drinker's attention. Barrio Blonde is a beer so light and tasty that fans can enjoy it all day, with no palate fatigue.

Borderlands Brewing Co.
Tucson

Beside the railroad tracks that slice their way through Tucson sits a century old brick structure – the rugged home of Borderlands Brewing Company. This historic location stands tall with bold charm, despite decades of Southern Arizona heat, storms, and heavy use. The inside is adorned with rustic finishes that blend right into the fading brick and wood. Massive beams cut across the roof, holding together one of the most beautiful taprooms in Arizona. Borderlands moved into the building in 2011, making this hyper-local brewery one of the first in town. Now, the two friends who started the business, Mike Mallozzi and Myles Stone, have elevated their beers to some of the state's most popular. Their winding journey started when Mike and Myles were reflecting on several highly successful homebrewing sessions, concluding that they were ready to go commercial. Since then, their growth has been rapid, all while supporting the neighborhood around them. Like any brewery worth its wort, the goal of Borderlands is to make delicious beer. At the same time, this brewery aims to do so while promoting sustainability and community. All the company's decisions are made with these principals in mind, right on down to water conservation and renewable energy efforts. Borderlands also takes pride in the cultural heritage of Tucson, so the founders do whatever they can to highlight the rich history of the area. Beers like the Noche Dulce nod to Tucson's Hispanic heritage by using ingredients like Mexican vanilla. Borderlands Brewing Company focuses on innovating beers to reflect the region. By collaborating with breweries like Sentinel Peak and sourcing ingredients indigenous to the area, Borderlands has created a truly local business.

Prickly Pear Wheat
Borderlands Brewing Company

ABV: 6.0%

IBU: 15

From the stunning color to the even more surprising flavor profile, this brew delivers a beer experience that visitors won't soon forget. The most exciting component of this recipe is the use of locally harvested prickly pear – giving this beer the spirit of the land. Fruit-infused beers are often overly sweet and juicy. That isn't so for this brew. In this recipe, the prickly pear is subtle yet present, resulting in an overall delectable beer. In order to get the perfect fruit to make this brew, Borderlands works directly with a local family-owned harvester. A close connection between the brewery and its supplier ensures that Borderlands will get a consistent product, matching what the recipe calls for. This local relationship with the fruit provider has been essential to the brewery's production of a sustainable, mouthwatering beer that incorporates an iconic regional ingredient. Borderlands requests the sweetest prickly pear juice, since the bright pink fruit isn't as saccharine as most people are led to believe. Because of the connection to Arizona, this brew fits right into Borderlands' lineup. Working in complement with the high wheat bill, prickly pear shapes this beer into a marvelous desert refreshment. Prickly Pear Wheat was one of the original flagship brews created by Borderlands, sticking around due to peoples' great response. Its fanbase has developed so much that the brewery is always cranking out new batches just to keep up with demand. The beer has passed beyond the taproom walls into distribution throughout Tucson, also making its way up to the Central Valley and Northern Arizona. When looking to pair Prickly Pear Wheat with food, lighter meals like salads or grilled chicken are ideal. Rich desserts like dark chocolate or cake also make a great match up.

Sentinel Peak Brewing Co.
Tucson

In January 2014, Sentinel Peak Brewing Company opened its doors – making it the first brewpub in Midtown Tucson. Two local firefighters, Jeremy Hilderbrand and Matt Gordon, created the brewery. Shortly after beginning the venture, the founding duo brought on Taylor Carter, also a firefighter, to round out the industrious team. From the very start, these three gentlemen were looking to create a family-oriented spot where craft beer drinkers could enjoy a comfortable atmosphere with delicious food and brews. So they built a brewing system piece-by-piece, drafted up a menu, and opened Sentinel Peak to the public. Once things got rolling, the growth came quickly. Sentinel Peak has now expanded to a second pub on the east side of town and a massive production facility that it shares with Borderlands Brewing Company. Not only has Sentinel Peak gained monumental traction down south, but its beers can be found across the state on tap and in eye-catching cans. The expansion didn't come without long hours and hard work, as the three founders are still active firefighters to this day. Because of that, it will be of no surprise that much of their business is inspired by their "day jobs." Imagery of firefighting pervades the Sentinel Peak brand, from axe-shaped tap handles to the skeletal red-and-white Salida Del Sol can art. Sentinel Peak's success story can largely be attributed to the owners' tenacity and a lineup of food and beers made to please virtually any palate. Popular German-inspired brews like 1811 Blonde and Dewpoint Dunkel fill the tap list as a result of Jeremy's passion for classic recipes. Loaded nachos, Sonoran tacos, and mesquite-smoked barbecue are just a handful of the menu items that pair great with a variety of Sentinel Peak beers.

Salida Del Sol

Sentinel Peak Brewing Company

ABV: 5.2%   IBU: 22

Several years ago, when Sentinel Peak was preparing to open its doors, its firefighting-founders were deciding just what types of beers they wanted to have on tap. One member of the group, Matt Gordon, was adamant about rolling out a Mexican Amber. So head brewer Jeremy Hilderbrand began to work on developing the perfect brew. Not before long, Jeremy poured his creation for Matt, who took a few sips and knew it was a stupendous beer. The recipe was named Salida Del Sol, or "sunrise" in Spanish, possibly because of the burnt amber color reminiscent of an early Arizona sky. Since its inception, Salida Del Sol has not had any major changes to the original recipe. These days, this Mexican-style beer has become the cornerstone of Sentinel Peak Brewing Company. Salida Del Sol has grown so much that it can be found in stores and on tap throughout Arizona. The style itself, a Mexican Amber, is almost exactly the same as a Vienna Lager, but with the addition of flaked corn. The Mexican Amber first came about after waves of German immigration to Mexico in the 19th century. The Germans who left Europe brought their world-famous love of beer and brewing along with them. The addition of flaked corn is the true differentiator in this beer, with its earthy, slightly vegetal impact on the overall flavor profile. Malt is the true star of this recipe, but the flaked corn adds significant nuance and surprise to the expected taste of a Vienna Lager. A sparing use of only noble hops keeps the malt and corn as the most recognizable components. When visiting Sentinel Peak, ask for the Salida Del Sol to be served with a lime wedge, which enhances the corn's earthy flavors.

Button Brew House

Tucson

Button Brew House is one of the most recent additions to the Tucson area's burgeoning craft beer community. Despite its youth, the brewery has managed to build a loyal customer base and land their beers into several different retail accounts. The taproom, open for just a couple years now, is an easy ten-minute drive north of downtown Tucson. Button is a comfortable, welcoming establishment with a giant window that gives patrons a view of the brewery's stainless-steel fermenters, where all the beer magic happens. Outside, a shade-covered patio sets a lowkey scene for visitors to kick back during the cooler seasons. Husband-and-wife founders Todd and Erika Button created the brewery to utilize their entrepreneurial experience in a way that would harness their passion. Before liftoff, the couple hadn't worked in a commercial brewery, but Todd had amassed a sizeable amount of homebrewing experience. He also spent years earning a formal brewing and business education all in the name of propelling his hobby into a business. Todd's years of preparation before opening the brewery were key in refining the various Button recipes. Most of Button's beers keep it classic, like the Button IPA and All Souls Stout. Still, Button pours less-common beers, including a fantastic spicy Chiltepin Red. Todd loves to explore the intersection of food and beer, giving him a special perspective when formulating recipes for his brew house. The wide range of styles available at Button make it an ideal setting for those looking to experience the many different flavors of beer. The sense of community at Button further enhances the experience for drinkers. Collaborative efforts with places like 1912 Brewing Company have brought Button right into the neighborhood mix.

Chiltepín Red
Button Brew House

ABV: 6.2%   IBU: 16

Chiltepíns are small, fiercely spicy peppers packed with smoky flavor and quickly fading heat. Of all the world's chile peppers, the chiltepín is the only one that originated within the United States. It has been harvested by Southwestern communities for countless years. This classic pepper has found an exciting new home in one of Button Brew House's most popular beers, Chiltepín Red. As a spice-forward red ale, this brew constantly pays homage to southern Arizona with its year-round presence on Button's tap list. The recipe was born in the early days of founder Todd Button's homebrewing sessions. Now, Button regulars and first timers alike find a thrilling experience in this unorthodox beer. The flavor profile of Chiltepín Red is spice forward, but its heat doesn't last as long as other chile-infused beers. A rapid fading spice intensity makes this brew much more palatable than expected. Chiltepín Red does bring a noticeable warmth when drinking, but not in an intrusive way. By adding the chiles at various points in the brewing process, Todd builds a nuanced spice character. Roasted caramel-like flavors from the malt give this beer a round and complex taste not too unfamiliar from a more typical red ale. Because of Chiltepín Red's controlled heat, Button Brew House often blends it with other beers like their All Souls Stout. Blending Chiltepín Red tamps down its spicy kick which pairs great with smooth, chocolatey beers or hoppy IPAs. Button also whips up micheladas with their beers on select days, allowing the Chiltepín's spicy taste to truly shine. Cooking food with Chiltepín Red is dynamite. The spicy yet deep, malty nature of the beer adds a layer of sophistication to any meal. Promising cooking options include marinating meats or making chili.

CRAFT BREWERY

1912

BREWING CO.

TUCSON ARIZONA

BREWING.COM | TUCSON, AZ

1912 Brewing Company
Tucson

When 1912 founder Allan Conger was enlisted in the United States Marine Corps, his service took him around the world. During his time overseas, he had the opportunity to try all sorts of regional beers. It was then, while sipping brews across the globe, that Allan developed a yearning to try homebrewing. Once he returned to the States, he started making his own beers. Allan spent a decade learning about the craft, honing his brewing techniques along the way. In 2015, Allan and his wife Alicia took their love of beer to the next level, opening 1912 Brewing Company in their native town of Tucson. From early on, 1912 latched on to sour beers, building out a tangy tap list filled with delectable diversity. Unsatisfied by simple recipes, Alan began producing increasingly creative combinations, no ideas being off-limits. As 1912 began to make a name for themselves by reinventing classic sours, unusual ingredients like saltwater taffy, Thai basil, and kimchi surfaced across the lineup of beers. To this day, the flavor explorations at 1912 extend far beyond delicious sour beers. From countless fruit infusions to the brewery's endless quest to research yeast and bacteria, 1912 is always innovating. Not only do they utilize unorthodox ingredients, 1912 also steps outside the typical boundaries of beer, easily pivoting to creations like hard seltzer. Collaborations frequently find a place on the brewery's tap list, as 1912 often teams up with beer producers from Arizona to as far as the east coast. As distribution expands, the sense of camaraderie will surely grow with it. The cozy 1912 tap room stands just a few minutes north of Downtown Tucson, but its beers can be found far from the brewery, with cans and kegs traveling across Arizona.

Naughty Naranja
1912 Brewing Company

ABV: 8.5%   IBU: 16

A few years ago, at a beer festival in Tucson, 1912 Brewing Company partnered with local firefighters to create a one-of-a-kind beer. The brewery's founder, Allan Conger, has a special place in his heart for sours, so he knew he wanted to brew the puckering style for the local event. At the time, 1912 was experimenting with different bacteria to use for fermentation, aiming to take their sours to the next level. While running some tests, Conger found that one of the cultures he isolated resulted in a beautifully strong natural orange flavor. Building from this, the crew at 1912 decided to add fruit to the recipe. The trick was finding the right fruit to accentuate the tropical esters from the bacteria. 1912 landed on an addition of blood oranges, playing off the flavors contributed by the proprietary culture. The brew was released to great fanfare and quickly won an award at a local beer festival. Naughty Naranja is a gose bursting with unexpected, complex flavors that can be appreciated even by non-beer-drinkers. With its heady ABV of 8.5%, the beer is a little trickier to produce than a typical gose, but its high velocity helps it stand out from the rest. Sea salt for the brew is harvested off the coast of La Jolla, California, known to produce some of the best salts in the U.S. Additions of toasted coriander give Naughty Naranja sumptuous herbal and citrus aromas, which weave perfectly into the beer. 1912 frequently explores creative changes to the recipe, including a 12% version brewed with tangerines. Other variations feature spices and peppers, making for a tantalizing alteration that pushes the style's limits. For those enjoying Naughty Naranja with a bite to eat, gravitate toward light seafood dishes.

Dillinger Brewing Company

Tucson

It shouldn't come as a shock that Dillinger Brewing Company, located just a few minutes from Downtown Tucson, was founded by two U of A alumni. What began as the typical late-night musings over drinks and cigars eventually morphed into one of Tucson's rising craft-beer stars. When Eric Sipe and Aaron Long opened Dillinger Brewing Company in late 2016, they were both in their mid-20s. With the help of talented head brewer John Ritter, the small business began to take off. Dillinger has begun to make a name in a city already ripe with several amazing craft breweries. Dillinger's collaborations with other local businesses, including a barrel swap program, have boosted their presence in the area and helped them gel with the Tucson craft community. Over the course of their growth Dillinger Brewing Company has become known for impressive flagships like Road Runner Red. They have also garnered excitement over eccentric concoctions, like Serrano Seduction, an American wheat spiked with chilies. Located right off Oracle Road, Dillinger Brewing Company has found the perfect place to serve their beers to the thirsty Tucson crowd. Their taproom, tucked in the back corner of a business park, pours creative brews in a room with speakeasy character. Since the brewery opened, patrons have eagerly shared the cozy spot with friends and family, helping to spread the word in a totally spontaneous manner. An almost guerilla-style approach to sharing their brews seems to be working. Many of Dillinger's beers, including the quirkier ones, are rapidly gaining traction in Tucson and throughout the state. Dillinger has truly hit its stride, and the crew is stoked to help represent an Arizona beer scene that, like them, is flourishing more every day.

Mango Nada
Dillinger Brewing Company

ABV: 5.7%   IBU: 10

In recent years, gose and other sour beers have quickly taken the industry by storm. This unique style has been around for hundreds of years, but has only recently experienced a resurgence within the American craft beer boom. One of Arizona's most exhilarating examples of a gose is the Mango Nada from Dillinger Brewing Company. Mango Nada has many classic components of a gose – like the use of a house lactobacillus strain to impart lush sour notes – while incorporating a handful of twists. By adding mango, tamarind, and a popular Mexican chili-lime seasoning to the recipe, Dillinger Brewing Company has created a highly unusual, delicious spin on this classic sour style. It took plenty of experimentation to come up with this concoction, but people have responded so well to the beer that Dillinger is working double time to keep up with demand. To achieve its signature flavor profile, Dillinger adds plenty of mango at different stages of brewing. While the various additions add a bit more work to the production process, they greatly increase the intensity and nuance of the juicy flavor. Adding mango early on allows some of the fruit to ferment with the wort. This special procedure builds layers of flavor while keeping the beer from becoming too saccharine. The seamless blending of sugary fruit and tartness from the lacto are what make this beer so special. When ordering Mango Nada at the Dillinger taproom, patrons will be served a glass coated in chili-lime seasoning. The spiced rim is reminiscent of a beachside margarita and even seems to make the Arizona heat a little more bearable. The salty and tart dimensions of Mango Nada make for a perfect match for seafood like fish tacos or grilled shrimp with lime marinade.

Tombstone Brewing Co.
Tombstone

The town of Tombstone is known for its rugged past and impassioned community that greatly appreciates the area's Wild West history. It can now also claim itself as home to one of Arizona's most respected craft beer producers. A few years ago, founder Matt Brown (pictured on the right) moved down from the Central Valley. Shortly after he arrived, Matt opened Tombstone Brewing Company on the edge of town, located inside of the old City Hall building. With the masterful recipes of head brewer Weedy Weidenthal (pictured on the left), Tombstone Brewing quickly caught the eyes of craft beer fans. While it may seem like a long way to drive for beer, Tombstone's edgy brewing projects have drawn in fans from around the state. Their beers have also won a variety of awards at competitions across the U.S. One of the biggest differentiators at Tombstone Brewing is an expansive barrel-aging program. Tombstone has set itself apart by producing a plethora of different barrel-aged styles, including more conventional imperial stouts, but also uncommon options like blonde ales. Some of the beers are even fermented directly inside the barrels. These brews are limited releases, usually available on draft and in bottles. Whether looking for a fruited Berliner Weisse, sweet barley wine, or flavorful double IPA, Tombstone brews are a must-try on the Arizona craft beer journey. With a constantly rotating tap list that ranges from lagers to sours, there is always something for everyone. A few of the brewery's most popular beers are its outstanding IPAs, including its New England styles that explode with delicious hop flavor and juiciness. It's difficult to find a brewery as innovative and daring as Tombstone that consistently produces amazing beverages.

Another Exercise in Mediocrity
Tombstone Brewing Company

ABV: 8.1%   IBU: 60

Most beers try to live up to their name. Luckily for Arizona craft beer fans, this isn't one of them. Infused with a bright charge of tropical hop flavors, Another Exercise in Mediocrity is a magnificent example of the big hazy IPAs that have blitzed the beer world in recent years – a style that has become Tombstone's signature. This beer is a double IPA, otherwise known as an imperial IPA, meaning that the alcohol content is significantly higher than a typical representation of the style. Another Exercise in Mediocrity hides its ABV firepower smoothly, making it almost dangerous. When enjoying Another Exercise in Mediocrity, consumers will immediately notice the sensational aroma that emanates from this beer. Potent and packed with hoppy fragrance, the drinkability factor of this brew is incredible. Its flavor profile is reminiscent of tropical fruit juice with a refreshing citrus pop. Getting a clean tropical taste with a slightly dank character is the key to making this beer so mouthwatering. To ensure its hops burst with freshness, Tombstone works directly with its hop growers. The brewery even goes as far as touring farms and picking specific hop lots to choose the perfect crop. Sourcing ingredients this way does introduce some minor inconsistencies, which wouldn't be as prevalent in more conventional hop batches, but it allows Tombstone to craft beers exactly how it wants them. With this beer, and many of its other double IPAs, Tombstone uses a malt bill that contributes just a mild flavor, keeping the central focus on the hops. Another Exercise's citrus-hop blast and high carbonation make it a great match for rich, fatty foods like cheeseburgers.

Icon Legend

 Produces cans or bottles

 Fills growlers or crowlers

 Has beer in distribution

 Has multiple locations

 At least one location is pet freindly

 At least one location has a patio

 At least one location has food trucks

 At least one location serves food

 At least one location is walking distance to another brewery

Glossary

ABV - Alcohol by volume. This measurement tells the alcoholic strength of a beer. Lighter beers typically have an ABV of about 4%, while stronger beers such as imperial stouts can be 10% or higher.

IBU - International Bitterness Units. This measurement indicates a beer's bitterness. Some beers, such as American lagers, typically have a lower IBU (10 to 20 IBUs), while IPAs have a higher IBU level (50 to 100 IBUs). When provided, the IBU number on beer menus can help consumers determine which beer to order.

Malt - A cereal grain that has been steeped, germinated, and dried for use in beer. Malt is typically barley, but brewers commonly use wheat and rye as well. The malting process creates the necessary environment within the grain for its sugars to be consumed by yeast during fermentation.

Hops - A flower that adds bitterness, flavor, and aromas to beer. Although sometimes the whole bud of the flower is used, hops are often concentrated into pellets for consistency, ease of use, and efficient storage. Aside from building flavor, aroma, and bitterness, hops have a major impact on prolonging a beer's shelf life.

Yeast - A microorganism responsible for the fermentation that makes beer possible. Yeast consumes sugars from the malt and converts them to alcohol and carbon dioxide. Before yeast was discovered, ancient beer makers thought of fermentation as magic from the gods. They weren't wrong!

Style Index

IPA

    480G by Beer Research Institute 85

    BOOM Dynamite by O.H.S.O. 45

    Downshift by Scottsdale Beer Company 73

    Mountains of Mosaic by Dark Sky Brewing Company 115

    Refuge by Arizona Wilderness Brewing Company 93

    Tower Station by Mother Road Brewing Company 107

Light Lager

    Day Drinker by Pedal Haus Brewery 61

Mead

    Berry White by Superstition Meadery 131

Mexican Amber

    Salida Del Sol by Sentinel Peak 161

Pale Ale

    Arizona Trail Ale by THAT Brewery 143

    Singularity Series by Oro Brewing Company 77

Style Index

Sour

Spice Beers

Stouts

Wheat Beer

About the Authors

Luke Irvin has a true love of creating educational and entertaining media, particularly when digging into the stories of people who inspire him. A photographer, videographer, and web developer, Luke uses his talents to create a wide range of content, frequently showcasing Arizona food and beer. Luke appreciates a delicious lager or dark, malty beer and always likes to pair his choice with a carefully crafted meal.

Eric Walters has been a fan of craft beer ever since he moved to Arizona in 2007. His passion for the great local scene led him to start Tap That AZ Podcast in 2017. A natural storyteller, his podcast highlights the people and stories behind the Arizona beer community. You can often find Eric enjoying a funky sour or farmhouse ale as he talks beer with a brewer, or a friend. When he isn't out enjoying Arizona beer, Eric spends time with his wife, Jackie, and two daughters, Kali and Cora.

Thank you for checking out The Arizona Beer Book Volume 1. We appreciate your support of our project and the Arizona craft beer scene. There are so many great breweries covered in the book, and many others beyond these pages. We highly encourage you to visit all of the places we have covered. Whether you live right up the street from one of the breweries, or have to make a trip to a neighboring town, there are so many local beers to try.

For more information check out our website, social media, and our YouTube page, which features multiple videos about some of the places covered in this book. Our website also has merchandise avaiable for purchase

www.TheArizonaBeerBook.com